The Winds of Turbulence

THE WINDS OF TURBULENCE

A CEO's Reflections on Surviving and Thriving on the Cutting Edge of Corporate Crisis

Howard D. Putnam

with

Gene Busnar

HarperBusiness

A Division of HarperCollins*Publishers*

Library of Congress Cataloging-in-Publication Data

Putnam, Howard D., 1937–
   The winds of turbulence: a CEO's reflections on surviving and
thriving on the cutting edge of corporate crisis/ Howard D. Putnam
with Gene Busnar.
      p. cm.
   Includes index.
   ISBN 0–88730–458–3
   1. Airlines—United States—Management.   2. United Air Lines.
inc.—Management.   3. Braniff Airways—Management.   4. Southwest
Airlines Co.—Management.   5. Chief executive officers—United
States.   6. Putnam, Howard D., 1937– .   I. Busnar, Gene.
II. Title.
HE9781.P88   1991
387.7'092—dc20   91–22284
[B]   .   CIP

Printed in the United States of America

91 92 93 94 CC/RRD 7 6 5 4 3 2 1

In memory of my parents, Virgil and Mary Putnam,
whose guidance and love in my formative years
on our Iowa farm provided an invaluable foundation . . .

And to my wife, Krista, and our children, Michael and Susan,
for being a great and supportive family team all these years.

Contents

Preface

"That's all for tonight. . . . I'm Robert MacNeil, goodnight."

It was May 11, 1983. I walked over to the TV, turned off the switch, and remarked to my wife, "Impressive." I had just seen and heard a stimulating MacNeil/Lehrer interview with Howard Putnam, one year after the Braniff Chapter 11 bankruptcy filing. And I truly was impressed.

Putnam had shared the story of his career at United, Southwest, and most recently Braniff. He had been direct, candid, and reflective about his leadership style, his motives in responding to Braniff's financial crisis, and his reasoning about various stakeholders (employees, customers, shareholders, creditors, etc.). "It's just a tremendous emotional roller coaster of ups and downs," he said. "The stress and the pressure are on you constantly because you have so many constituencies."

I had been on the Harvard Business School faculty for three years by this time and was actively developing business ethics cases and other materials for the MBA curriculum. Since an educator in the field of business ethics has to be a careful listener, I paid close attention to the way Putnam described his experience. Over the years, a teacher develops a sixth sense for potentially valuable learning tools. Howard Putnam's interview on MacNeil/Lehrer convinced me that there was a good case study here if Putnam would "sit" for it.

It was important to me and to my students that the ethical dimensions of executive thinking be examined with as much realism as idealism. Here was a CEO describing in some detail an extraordinarily challenging decision-making process, and describing it in a way that evidenced instinctive moral concern for the affected parties.

The next morning, I asked my secretary to try to get a telephone number for Howard Putnam in Dallas, Texas. Putnam was as easygoing on the phone as he was in the TV interview. I explained my interest in doing a Harvard case study of the Braniff bankruptcy. I wanted to reconstruct for MBA students and executives some of the decisions that he had to make, with special emphasis on the ethical aspects of those decisions. If I were to send my assistant to Dallas, would he be willing to give interview time and other information to make a good case? Some business leaders needed a lot of reassurance about casewriting before they would consider it. But Putnam knew firsthand what Harvard cases were like and this made the "sell" easier. He agreed to participate. I put the phone down and went over to Baker Library to gather electronically a list of articles and abstracts on Braniff over the past five years. I then called my research assistant, David Whiteside, and told him that I had an idea for a case research effort on the ethics of leadership in a bankruptcy situation. We met a day later.

We wrote the case over the next several months and invited Putnam, Phil Guthrie, and their wives to visit Harvard on the day it was first taught. The case was quite successful. Students wrestled with Putnam's decisions and actions as he and Guthrie took over the reins at Braniff, started making changes, faced cash crisis after cash crisis, and communicated with employees, unions, creditors, and media. These future leaders struggled with "honesty vs. results" questions as Howard Putnam listened from the back row "sky deck" in the classroom. We videotaped Putnam's interaction with the students that day and used it in subsequent years when the case was taught. It was (and continues to be) an excellent learning tool.

That's how I came to know Howard Putnam. Before I got to know him as a friend, he was for me a window on the mind of an effective and ethically sensitive business leader. He let you in on his thought processes in ways that were valuable and rare for executives.

He was a counter-example, as I saw it, to the thesis in Michael Maccoby's 1976 book, *The Gamesman.* Maccoby argued that to get to positions of leadership in large corporations, a person had to sacrifice traits of the "heart" (compassion, generosity, idealism) in favor of traits of the "head" (efficiency, goal-directedness, innovativeness). The natural selection at work in the modern business organization favored not balance, but single-minded determination, not wholeness but partiality.

Putnam sounded different to me when I first heard him—no stereotype here. He was as comfortable talking about strategy and the ingredients of successful competition as he was talking about honesty, integrity, and fairness. He was the kind of leader who could be tough at the negotiating table and yet join his baggage handlers for a day or so working side by side to demonstrate solidarity, as he did in the Braniff case.

Ethics, I am convinced, has to do with the cognitive and emotional patterns by which individuals and organizations respond to challenges or conflicts. For some leaders (Type 1), the response is purely strategic, purely geared toward self-interest or winning competitive advantage. The way they scan the environment, sort out issues, synthesize data, plan action, and learn from experience is driven solely by economic gain.

Other leaders (Type 2) go beyond economic gain—but stop short of full-blooded ethical motivation. For them, the law is the fundamental touchstone. Compliance with regulation and legislation becomes a surrogate for conscience.

Finally, there are leaders (Type 3) who guide their own conduct and their organization's by values or principles that go beyond economic gain and legal compliance. Putnam struck me as such a leader, and his handling of the Braniff crisis was a case in point, for he was confronted with concerns on many fronts: employees needed straight talk; ticket holders and agents did too; shareholders and creditors had much at risk. These were for Putnam not just economic or legal claimants; they were real people with real stakes to whom he owed real obligations.

The challenge of Type 3 leadership in large, publicly held corporations is not small. For one thing, there are strong incentives to focus on short-term, quantifiable results. There are also strong *dis*incentives against factoring in the rights and interests of non-stockholders, at least if they are in tension with bottom-line results. Laws in most states, while they take precedence over corporate interests, also make it difficult for managers and directors to let anything else take precedence. Type 3 leaders who march to a *third* drum (ethical values that go beyond law-governed profit) are at the edge of legitimacy even though they are simply recognizing the limits of Types 1 and 2.

Sometimes the economic calculations are either vague or short-term. And the legal considerations are neutral or permissive. At such times, it takes courage to face potential criticism and to opt for such virtues as fairness or environmental protection or honesty, virtues that Howard Putnam emphasizes in his reflections on leadership.

The corporate leader who balances economic competition, legal compliance, and moral responsibility imposes upon self and company a fuller agenda than the leader concerned only with profitability and legality.

When I do lectures and workshops on business ethics, I like to emphasize that there are three levels of application that are important and interactive: the person, the organization, and the social system. A person must have character before he or she can confer this quality on an organization through leadership. Nobody gives what he or she doesn't have.

Similarly, an organization must have certain values before it can (through living or dying) confer them on the capitalistic system. It is sometimes sad to see a company go under or reorganize, but if the process is led with intelligence and integrity, it can actually strengthen the system and value the stakeholders at the same time.

Howard Putnam shares himself as a person in this book. And he shares his philosophy of moving from personal to organizational values. Finally, he shares his respect for the system as a whole, even when it is not hospitable to an organization's struggle to survive. Readers will benefit from sharing his journey, especially those who seek a more reflective and responsible leadership role.

Kenneth E. Goodpaster
Koch Professor of Business Ethics
University of St. Thomas
Minneapolis/St. Paul, Minnesota
March 15, 1991

Acknowledgments

For their encouragement and support of this project, I will always be grateful

- to Krista, my wife, for giving me the impetus to start this book and for constant feedback on the material presented.

- to our son, Michael, an airline captain, and his wife, Robin, a flight attendant, for their constant questioning of facts and figures.

- to our daughter, Susan, a free-lance writer, photographer, and producer, for her many helpful suggestions on approach and content.

- to Zig Ziglar, the great speaker, teacher, author, and friend, who said, "You have walked your talk. Now put it in writing and try to help others."

- to Dr. Don E. Beck, founder of the National Values Center in Denton, Texas, whose constant input and availability to assist me in matching theory, intuition, and just plain logic has been invaluable. Much of the turbulence theory discussed in this book came out of his research practice over the years with corporations and societies in the United States and South Africa.

- to Dr. Kenneth Goodpaster, the father of ethics at the Harvard Graduate School of Business Administration for his excellent case study on Braniff, "The Ethics of Bankruptcy," which examined how balanced values are necessary in crisis situations.

- to the late Garvin Lally, for developing the original proposal for this book and for his many hours of productive work in making it a reality.

- to Jeff Herman, my literary agent and friend, whose honesty, sincerity, and faith kept me believing there really was a story to be told.

- to the late Edward E. Carlson, former chief executive officer of Westin Hotels and United Airlines, for being the kind of "people person" mentor and leader that left such an impression on me.

- to the Reverend Bill Carr of Grace Presbyterian Church in Plano, Texas, where we reside, for always making himself available for a quick lunch to discuss a premise or an ethical issue.

- to all the employees at Southwest Airlines and Braniff International, who were so loyal and provided friendship and support through the good times and those times more difficult and stressful. They exemplified the true meaning of "customer service."

- to Virginia Smith, my executive editor at HarperCollins, for encouraging and keeping this novice author on track.

- to Jamie Forbes, for his invaluable feedback and assistance in editing the chapters.

- and to Gene Busnar, for taking all my hours of audio tapes, notes, stories, and a draft manuscript, and writing a book that sounds like me. That is the work of a professional writer and a real accomplishment.

Author's Note

Dear Reader,

This book is the product of over thirty years of experiences in businesses small and large. They range from the farm, service station, and grocery store in Bedford, Iowa, to small and large airlines across the United States . . . And from successes and dead ends in entrepreneurial experiences to a great feeling of inner satisfaction from being able to put back a little into civic and not-for-profit enterprises. If you can walk away from reading this book with one small tip that will improve your opportunities for business and personal improvement, and a greater feeling of well-being about yourself, then my mission will have been fulfilled.

Howard D. Putnam

The Winds of Turbulence

1

Get Ready for Anything: The Preflight Checklist

We live in erratic times. We fly in turbulent business skies. In the past few years we have seen more dramatic political and economic shifts in the world than have occurred in all the decades since World War II. Some of these shifts have already affected our businesses; others will make themselves felt in the future—and nobody can predict with any certainty just how.

As the world's business environment continues to undulate relentlessly, success will depend on our ability to channel the raw energy of this turbulence in productive and profitable ways.

I have long used the term *turbulence* to describe the agitation that is a constant in business. These unsettling winds are felt more acutely today than ever before.

The concept of turbulence is one most commonly associated with aviation, and it is no coincidence that I have spent most of my working life in this field. Nevertheless, I can think of no better term to portray the sudden, frequently unexpected, movement that characterizes the environment in which we all do business.

I first entered the corporate world in the 1950s, and I have seen much change in the years since then. Those changes occasionally have been so severe that they have produced what some have called chaos. In my view, though, change becomes chaotic only when it is not harnessed to fruitful ends.

Within any environment, there are areas of calm, agitation,

opportunity, and danger—as well as areas of unknown risks. Because of these coexisting but conflicting elements, all environments are turbulent. As individuals and as corporations, our decisions and our actions create some of the turbulence in our environments. However, even the most influential person is but one factor in the societal environment, and the largest corporations are only pieces of the total global business environment. Seen from this perspective, it is not hard to understand why most turbulence is the creation of aggregate forces that are largely outside our control.

Although we cannot eliminate turbulence from business or from any other environment, we can do much to harness its considerable power. Once we are aware of the nature of turbulence, we can prepare for it by developing the skills and the courage to weather it—and even to make it work for us. My primary purpose in writing this book is to arm you with those skills and that courage.

In strict business terms, turbulence is unexpected change in such areas as revenue, profits, the labor pool, investor interest, cost of equipment, sales, consumer tastes, market size, and the effects of competition. As leaders of companies, we can prepare for the unknown by building tightly integrated yet highly flexible organizations that are adept at harnessing turbulence productively in the business environment. Or we can build rigid fortresses of bureaucratic power that defend the one true way to do things—the way they are presently being done.

Throughout these pages, I draw heavily on my diverse experiences at United, Southwest, and Braniff airlines to illustrate the choices that are available in both good and bad times for dealing with various kinds of turbulence.

Four Flight Paths

Every company has the potential to follow four basic flight paths. Imagine that your business is an airplane. From the outset, the business can face four possible futures:

1. A company begins at a certain point, proceeds from there, inevitably experiences difficulty, effectively manages the

difficulty, and ultimately reaches a new starting point. Then it starts a new cycle—the nature of which is always unknown.

This is the typical path of a company that is prepared for turbulence. It responds to difficulty by maximizing all its resources, making some mistakes, learning from them, and then proceeding at a more advanced level than before.

2. A company begins at a certain point, proceeds, inevitably experiences difficulty, and manages that difficulty in an ineffective manner—causing problems to escalate to more serious levels.

   In time, the company finds a solution, enters a fragile state of rebirth, fully reestablishes itself, and ultimately reaches a new starting point. Then it begins another cycle—which is always unknown.

3. A company begins at a certain point, proceeds, inevitably experiences difficulty, and ineffectively manages that difficulty—causing problems to escalate to more serious levels.

   In time, the company finds a solution, enters a fragile state of rebirth, is overcome by regrowing pains, slips back into crisis, and finally ceases to exist.

4. A company begins at a certain point, proceeds, inevitably experiences difficulty, and ineffectively manages that difficulty. Problems escalate to unmanageable levels, and the company ceases to exist.

These paths are just small segments of the much larger, multicyclical courses all companies take. Keep this model in mind as you continue to read. Think about the path that your company is following at this time and the direction it is taking. The particular path a company takes depends on many things, including the following:

- The state of turbulence in the environment in which the company does business
- The state of the local, national, and global economies
- The general health of the industry in which the company participates
- The state of the competition

- Employee morale and productivity
- Consumer loyalty
- Prices of supplies, raw materials, and energy
- The cost of securing capital

Various combinations of these factors can significantly influence the type and amount of turbulence a business experiences. And although there may not be a way to prevent some of these occurrences, virtually all of them can be managed to productive and profitable ends. As these pages reveal, quality of management ultimately determines the path a company takes.

I have found that six states of turbulence strongly affect a company's destiny. As you will see, however, a company's fate is not determined solely by the kinds of winds that are blowing. The difference between success and failure most often comes down to a single question: how good are the folks who are piloting the proverbial airplane at harnessing and controlling those winds?

Alpha State: Forward Turbulence

When a company is in Alpha* state, it is metaphorically experiencing clear skies and smooth sailing. In this state, a company is successfully addressing the challenges, risks, opportunities, and problems of business. The company is in its niche: it is satisfying the needs of customers, employees, lenders, and shareholders—all constituents who have a stake in its welfare.

An Alpha company is maximizing its resources. It has a low turnover of personnel and a steady increase in earnings and profit. Product quality and innovation are high. Inventory is low, and so are customer complaints. Companies in Alpha are financially and spiritually prosperous. They are having fun and making money at it. They are contributing dollars to research and development. At the same time, they are giving something

*Note: The terms *Alpha, Beta, Gamma,* and *Omega* are derived from international communications codes. They were originally used by industrial psychologist Dr. Don Beck to describe various turbulent states in business.

back to the community through donations and volunteerism. Alpha companies reconcile economic growth with the welfare of the environment.

More often than not, an Alpha company is operating in a favorable general business environment. Interest rates tend to be stable, unemployment low, and inflation below 4 percent. Although such external factors make it easier for a company to remain in Alpha state, they are not absolutely necessary. A superbly led company can be in Alpha even in desperate economic times.

There is no time limit on how long a company can remain in Alpha. Some companies pass immediately through Alpha to another less productive and less harmonious state. Some stay in Alpha for extended periods. The goal is to stay in Alpha for as long as possible. A company in Alpha is free from the turbulence of mistakes. (Of course it is also free from the benefit of learning from such mistakes, which, ironically, could have a negative effect in the long run.)

To remain in Alpha for any length of time, a company must be vigilant in nine specific areas. These are the nine basic steps a business must take to stimulate growth and ensure ongoing prosperity:

1. *Promote the team concept.* A company must be committed to developing and maintaining balanced management teams—complementary groups possessing the skills and values that underlie stability and growth. These skills include creativity, intellect, stamina, and tolerance. Some of these values are integrity, loyalty, compassion, courage, and altruism. The unique kind of teamwork necessary for maintaining an Alpha state is detailed in Chapter 2, Nobody Flies Solo: Building the Senior Management Team.

2. *Fulfill constituent needs.* A company that does not address the real and perceived needs and desires of all constituent groups—employees, customers, lenders, shareholders, trade suppliers—will quickly slip into a state less productive than Alpha. Rewarding constituent groups—particularly employees—is discussed in Chapter 3, What's in It for Me? Fulfilling Employee Dreams.

3. *Eliminate bureaucracy.* To reduce bureaucracy within an organization, a company must excise unnecessary management layers and cut down on task redundancy. A company should reperceive its structure as one linked by common values and goals instead of one based on hierarchy and command. Reducing bureaucracy is discussed in Chapter 4, The Putnam Principle of Organizational Gravity.

4. *Maintain simplicity.* A company that wishes to stay in an Alpha state must keep its mission, strategy, and tactics simple. This is covered in Chapter 5, In 100 Words or Less: Keep Your Strategy Short, Sweet, and Simple.

5. *Contain costs.* A company must discipline its expenses. Budgets should not constitute a license to spend. Achievement should be motivated by productivity rather than by spending. A detailed discussion on the subject of controlling costs can found in Chapter 6, The $27,000 Cocktail: Contain Costs—At All Costs.

6. *Have fun.* A company that wishes to extend its stay in Alpha must be enthusiastic about its business. Otherwise, boredom takes root, and with boredom come carelessness, negligence, and eventual abuse. Having fun and creating enthusiasm in the workplace are discussed in Chapter 7, Are We Having Fun Yet? It Takes More Than Just a Paycheck.

7. *Make a commitment to ethical behavior.* A company that fails at ethics ultimately fails at business. The 1980s produced scores of examples of how lax ethics brought down many individuals and some huge companies. A strong ethical stance is at least as powerful as any other single factor in helping a company remain in Alpha. Company value systems are discussed in the Chapter 8, Follow the Yellow Brick Rule: Seven Golden Roads to Corporate Virtue.

8. *Build frequent and open reciprocal communication into the fabric of your company.* Most of the above issues depend on regular and candid communication. Teams and constituents need to communicate; ethical behavior and fun are achieved through communication, as are reductions in bureaucracy and control of costs.

As essential as constant communication is for Alpha companies to maintain that state, it is especially important for companies mired in less productive and less harmonious states as they struggle to achieve a new Alpha. The specifics of maintaining open communication links with employees and customers are detailed in Chapter 9, Open the Kimono! The Ten Commandments of Crisis Communication.

9. *Always remain flexible and adaptive.* A company that intends to remain in Alpha must be chameleon-like in its ability to adapt to changes in its surroundings. There is never only one way to do things. Flexibility is probably the key to navigating and surviving the winds of turbulence we are sure to experience for the remainder of the 1990s and well into the twenty-first century.

Once you understand the basics of growth and survival that are explored in these pages, you will have the tools to solve problems creatively.

I learned a great deal about the importance of flexibility and adaptiveness during my tenures with Southwest and Braniff. Southwest was in an Alpha state during almost the entire time I was that company's CEO. This was partly due to my influence, but most of the credit must go to the senior management team that guided the airline from being an $80 million entrepreneurial venture to be a $240 million regional competitor.

Southwest remained in Alpha because it paid intense attention to the nine issues that promote business growth and prosperity. The company was especially good at using its people as early warning systems. Employees, particularly those on the front line, are a company's pulse—and its most valuable source of intelligence.

Speaking of early warning systems, I'd like to share a chilling story of an airplane that nearly slipped out of Alpha and straight into chaos. The overnight cargo flight of a major airline was en route from New York to Los Angeles. The weather was clear, and the pilots had flown the route many times. Everything was proceeding smoothly. In fact, the entire event was a perfect model of the Alpha state—smooth, steady progress.

It is not unusual to turn on the autopilot in the course of such flights—especially when they take place in the middle of the night during periods of light air traffic and stable weather conditions. After all, there is not much to worry about—or is there? On this particular night, with the autopilot handling the cockpit, the crew fell asleep. This kind of complacency, of course, is extremely dangerous—not only to airplane pilots but to every man and woman who affects the destiny of an Alpha company.

Ten miles or so past Los Angeles International Airport, the control tower tried to call the cockpit. As the airplane headed farther and farther out over the Pacific Ocean, the air traffic control people continued their attempts to reach the airplane over the radio—but with no response. Although the pilots still did not realize it, they had moved into a new state of turbulence—and potential catastrophe.

One hundred miles over the Pacific, the crew finally responded to the SELCALL, a selective emergency call directed to a specific airplane that sets off an alarm. It awakened the crew, which was promptly informed that the plane was 100 miles off course. At that point, the pilot turned the plane around.

Fortunately, in this instance the crew responded in time, and the flight remained in Alpha. Yet that plane was on the brink of disaster.

Companies in Alpha must be ready for anything if they intend to maintain that lofty state. The way to do that is to stay alert—in effect, to assume a crisis mentality before a critical situation can overtake you. This is a challenge when things appear to be going well.

The forward motion of a company in Alpha state can be easily disrupted by perturbations in the business environment, unless those perturbations are managed and harnessed to fruitful ends. For Braniff Airlines, deregulation was a wind shift that the company's leaders misperceived as an opportunity for unprecedented expansion. Deregulation was a perturbation in the business environment that could have boosted Braniff's fortunes. But because its leadership failed to navigate these winds of turbulence correctly, deregulation sent Braniff reeling.

Prior to deregulation, Braniff was in an excited Alpha state. I'll never forget the evening I met Harding Lawrence, the CEO who threw Braniff into its tailspin. Nor will I forget the piercing determination in his eyes as he spoke of the airline's future. As he talked of his vision for Braniff, I felt that I was looking at someone who was engulfed by the grandness of his fantasy. It was also clear that Harding Lawrence *was* Braniff. Instead of being navigated by a balanced and flexible team, Braniff's fortunes depended on one man. Lawrence's magnificent dream of Braniff's future would either make the airline the free world's largest carrier or send it tail over nose into chaos.

Less than one year after Harding and I met, Braniff was out of control. I was the person called in to save that floundering airline.

Beta State: Resistive Turbulence

A company in Beta state experiences agitation, irritation, and discomfort. The turbulence it encounters impedes its forward movement. The first signs of trouble come into view: the wind picks up or changes direction; clouds appear overhead; a little rain starts to fall; a storm front is spied on the horizon. A company in Beta may experience any or all of the following: discord among its employees, increased customer complaints, decreased investor interest, lack of cooperation from suppliers, a slip in market share, a dip in profits.

Such shifts in the winds of turbulence often occur when the reality of the environment does not match that forecast by the company. Interest rates are supposed to go down, but instead, they go up. Product *X* is supposed to be shipped by December, but because of unforeseen delays, it ships in June. The executive vice president in charge of operations is supposed to be a loyal employee, but unexpectedly, he takes a higher-paying position with the competition.

Surprisingly, it is not unusual for a Beta state to occur after a company has had tremendous success. Sometimes, Beta is the simple result of boredom. As the plane crew that fell asleep during a smooth flight learned, it is tempting to become complacent when everything appears to be going well.

When a company's leaders rest on their laurels, turbulence often is created through their neglect. When those same leaders become cocky and arrogant, they can create turbulence through increased staff friction. When the men and women piloting an Alpha company drop their guard and grow lazy in their vigilance, Beta walks in.

As a rule, Beta occurs when the game changes in some way but the players continue to play the way they always have. Soon after entering Beta, a company feels those turbulent winds and recognizes that something is wrong. At that point, it can take three approaches to reestablish order.

MORE OF THE SAME

A company's first response to trouble often is to do more of the same. It hunkers down and works harder and faster at what it has been doing all along. Leaders ask their teams to put their noses to the grindstone; teams ask their staffs to get with the program. Everything is done with the mistaken belief that what has been practiced in the past should still be practiced—just more intensely. After all, people reason, it used to work, so why shouldn't it still work?

Unfortunately, by the time a company finds itself in Beta, more of the same only exacerbates existing turbulence. Leaders tend to throw money and people at problems—yet those problems persist. As a result, frustration grows and morale slips, while conflict and discord deepen.

FIRST-ORDER CHANGE: REFORM

At this point in Beta, leaders and employees try to retune or renovate the corporate machine. Senior management makes adjustments. Middle management recognizes bad habits and changes them. The front line gets a pep talk. Sometimes this approach works—but only for a while.

The adjustments and pep talks that take place as customer complaints continue to increase and revenues continue to fall may create a bright spot—a blip of improvement. However, because such changes do not address the underlying causes of the trouble, things often become worse than they were before the retuning. The problems encountered in Beta are usually too sweeping to be repaired by retuning, renovating, or refurbishing. At this stage, reforms simply are not enough.

Refurbishing a company experiencing Beta-level stress is a change of the first order. It is an attempt to make alterations within a system without changing that system. This approach is doomed to fail because the cosmetic changes on which it relies are inadequate for repairing substantial problems.

When fixing bits and pieces of a problematic system does not work, companies tend to wax nostalgic. Leaders of companies, heads of divisions, and their respective employees look backward—to those good old days when everything always ran smoothly.

At this point, companies sometimes try to recreate the past, but this approach almost never works. The old ways were discarded because they ceased being effective. At one point, the old ways ran their course, and change created progress. Beta is a sign that a company's most recent ways are no longer functional.

Once again, it is time to institute substantial new changes. In the midst of the perturbations generated by Beta, however, companies fail to see that history is repeating itself. Then, suddenly, something clicks.

SECOND-ORDER CHANGE: REFRAME

Change of the second order occurs when a company's leaders realize that the system within which a company, division, or department operates needs to be examined. At that point, a light of recognition goes on. Once a company recognizes and begins to address systemwide problems, new openings are created. These openings are the windows through which a company moves out of Beta state. This is reframing.

For reframing to occur, a company must have *flex*—that is, the ability to adapt to changes in its environment. Flex allows a company to recognize and exercise the *evolutionary option*—the stepping stone that leads to a more productive and harmonious state of operation.

Flex and the Evolutionary Option

A company's flex is its readiness to accept change—its willingness and ability to respond to the turbulence within its environment.

High-flex companies spend more time in Alpha than in other states because they constantly shift their attention to meet the challenges of the turbulence around them.

In the early 1980s two perturbations created turbulence for the entire airline industry: jet-fuel prices increased dramatically, and the federal government deregulated the airline industry. The different ways that Southwest and Braniff responded to the same wind shifts are instructive.

Because it was a high-flex company, Southwest was able to meet the challenge of increased jet-fuel prices quickly. We added a small department to manage any extreme changes that might occur. We also adapted our operations to meet external influences beyond our control. For example, we did not add new jets to our fleet as soon as we had intended. Other fuel-conservation measures included canceling low-occupancy flights, flying at slower speeds, and shutting down one engine while taxiing on the ground.

Deregulation in conjunction with higher fuel prices also created some interesting problems and opportunities for Southwest. We did seek to add new routes, but we took care to maintain our niche as a regional carrier that offered its customers an attractive alternative to lower-cost forms of transportation.

High-flex companies are able to adapt to meet the challenges of an undulating environment. Low-flex companies hang on to the old—to what is perceived as reliable, stable, and necessary. Low-flex companies are very much like the proverbial square pegs trying to squeeze into round holes.

Braniff was a reasonably flexible company up to the time the airline industry was deregulated. Then it dropped the ball.

Deregulation was a perturbation that caused turbulence in Braniff's operating environment—turbulence to which it responded quickly, but ineffectively and unwisely. Braniff's leaders, particularly its then-CEO, Harding Lawrence, responded to deregulation with an ill-perceived vision of the future. He thought the industry would become reregulated very quickly, but he was wrong. This is the danger of flying solo.

As I illustrate more fully in later chapters, Braniff continued on a course designed for a reregulated industry and eventually collapsed. As with Southwest, increased oil prices also created a perturbation for Braniff. But instead of adapting to the changes in the environment, the airline continued to expand and expand and expand. It was a time for all airlines to rethink jet-fuel consumption, but Braniff stubbornly proceeded as if what had always worked before would continue to work.

For Braniff and Southwest, deregulation and rising oil prices were sources of increased turbulence in their operating environments. Braniff approached both deregulating and increased oil prices with abandon and old paradigms, thus providing a quintessential example of acute low flex. Through a high degree of flexibility, Southwest turned deregulation and increased oil prices to its benefit. It carefully calculated opportunities and rethought its management of resources. It also exhibited most of the qualities that characterize high-flex companies:

- Courageous, "beginner's mind" leadership—the type of fresh and open thinking that encourages people to keep learning, even as they are teaching others
- Balanced, democratic management teams
- Relatively flat, less bureaucratic organizations with simple missions, strategies, and tactics
- Long-view, broad-scope thought—the kind that dispenses with instant gratification and concentrates on building for the future
- Tight, practical financial controls that encourage productivity, not padding
- Team spirit and enthusiasm for service
- Incentives for contributions by all constituents—including employees, customers, lenders, suppliers, and investors
- Open, honest, and congruent communication
- Impeccable ethical standards and empowering value systems

These characteristics are fully explored in later chapters. All are indicators of the kind of high-flex approach a company needs to find an evolutionary option out of Beta.

The evolutionary option allows a company to resolve its problems so it can move from its current situation to a more fruitful and peaceful state and to new possibilities. Evolutionary options can be either discovered within an organization or presented from the outside.

Internal evolutionary options are driven by a commitment to a new future from the CEO, the senior management team, and, ideally, all employees. This future is realized through maximizing the potential of a company's human resources—by tapping into the creativity, intellect, pride, and enthusiasm of its people. Out of this unrealized potential often come the information, capital, technology, and human resources needed to move a company out of the troubled Beta state.

Systemic changes within a company are often prompted by external influences. Beta can be resolved when the board requests a new CEO or when there is a companywide consolidation of effort. Sometimes lenders or investors increase support, and consultants recommend new patterns of behavior and new policies. Occasionally, competitive intelligence reveals a novel way of approaching a problem.

Ultimately, a company's degree of flex is the critical factor in determining the impact of the Beta state. If a company has low flex, the turbulent winds of Beta can cause it to move toward even more dangerous and destructive conditions. On the other hand, that same turbulence can move a high-flex company toward renewed possibilities and opportunities. For entities in a state of high flex, the evolutionary option creates a surgical change that generates new strength and an opportunity to rise to a new plateau.

New Alpha State: Renewed Forward Turbulence

A company that successfully comes through Beta enters a state of New Alpha. Although New Alpha resembles Alpha, the context is different. External conditions may be pretty much the same as they were the first time around, but the game has been altered because the company acquired new skills while it was in Beta. Nevertheless, the key to success in New Alpha is the same as it was in Alpha—constant vigilance on all fronts and maximized use of all resources.

One danger that companies face in New Alpha is being lulled to sleep by a false sense of security. A company's leaders may feel that they have reached the top of the roller coaster because they've passed the acid test of Beta, but the nature of the ride means that valleys eventually follow peaks. If you and your company are going to withstand the winds of turbulence, one of the most serious mistakes you can make is allowing yourself to feel too secure. The homeostasis of New Alpha is an illusion. More often than not, in a turbulent business environment, comfort and success mask impending tumult.

The above cautions notwithstanding, any company that musters the resources to move from Beta into New Alpha is on the road to greater success. On the other hand, a company that cannot withstand the challenges of Beta will fall deeper into pandemonium.

Gamma State: Chaotic Turbulence

A company in Gamma has hit rock bottom. The kind of chaos engendered in such circumstances can be compared to the swirling of dry leaves in a hurricane. Frustration has reached explosive levels. Antisocial behavior—in terms of the corporate society—sets in, as does self-destructive behavior. Thievery, embezzlement, and even sabotage may occur. Morale disintegrates. Resources either freeze up or become unmanageable due to internal disarray or outside influence. Options flitter away. Integrity crumbles. Hostility festers. Annihilative momentum grows.

In Gamma, it is much too late for minor adjustments. It is also too late for evolution. In a political situation, Gamma state may lead to violence, armed rebellion, destruction, and death. Unless radical measures are put into place, companies that find themselves in a comparable state of chaos will cease to exist.

The implosive-explosive nature of Gamma forces individuals to choose between two options: either quit, or else smash through barriers with every bit of creativity, intelligence, and will they can gather. Although the new application of existing resources can lead a company in Beta into New Alpha, such measures will not work in Gamma: the turbulent winds have catapulted the entity to the brink of disaster, and survival is possible only by applying previously unknown resources.

A company in Gamma must regenerate itself, or it will perish. Regeneration means that a company must redefine its basic mission, its strategy, and its tactics. Its leaders must completely rethink their commitment to all constituents as well as their handling of communications and financial obligations.

A corporation engulfed in Gamma must transform itself from an entity that is disintegrating to a new entity that is genetically different from the old. The reborn entity must be suitable to the environment in which it operates. If weak ethics and value systems contributed to the company's slide into Gamma, then leadership must correct them without delay.

The process of rescuing a company from Gamma is anything but easy, yet it is far from impossible. The tools in this book can be used preventively to help you avoid Gamma, but if you find yourself in that tenuous state, you can anticipate encountering some fairly predictable problems.

The barriers conspiring to stop a company from successfully negotiating Gamma are both real and imagined. In a sense, there is no difference between a real barrier, such as an unfavorable economy, and an imagined barrier, such as fear of an unknown future. Both have the same effect: they halt progress. Barriers need not be dead ends, however. Think of them as castle walls: they are very high and difficult to scale, but they have another side.

Fear is the most imposing barrier to transformation. Fear flows from the feelings of instability caused by dealing with the unknown, and it can strangle creative thinking. In later stages of Gamma, fear—almost always accompanied by anger—can result from

1. Knowing what is wrong
2. Knowing why it is wrong
3. Knowing what it will take to move out of Gamma and into New Alpha.

When a company passes through these stages of Gamma and arrives at the final stage, the proverbial light of recognition has flashed, and it is on the verge of exercising a revolutionary option. However, the barriers that remained to be scaled and smashed may be numerous and massive.

When the Braniff board board invited me to transform that company, it knew what was wrong, why it was wrong, and what had to be done. For Braniff, I was the revolutionary option. As the new CEO, I opened up communications, formed a powerful senior management team, slashed bureaucracy, simplified planning, assumed control of expenditures, generated a new sense of urgency, and transfused a new value system into the failing airline. As the result of a strong joint effort on the part of the new management team and all of Braniff's constituents, we were able to surmount or shatter all remaining barriers—including bankruptcy—until the airline flew again.

A company in Gamma is very much like an airplane that has encountered a wind shear while landing. In order to avert disaster, a company must focus all its energy on the immediate question of surviving the wind shear before it can again concentrate on landing. At the same time, the leaders who are piloting that company must never lose sight of their ultimate goal—to land.

This is the mindset of Gamma: energy is wholly directed toward problems but with an eye toward the long-term goals necessary to ensure the future. As you can imagine, Gamma is not a day at the beach. Then again, revolutions never do come easy.

Omega State: Expansive, Nondirected Turbulence

Omega is the delicate state that follows a successful revolution. The internal turbulence in Omega is expansive and non-directed—like a sun radiating energy in all directions at once. Even with tremendous dynamism and intensity, the rebirth of a company is always more fragile than its birth. There is a euphoria akin to having come through the worst of a storm. There is also exuberance and relief, great expectations, and raw, powerfully enthusiastic energy.

In Omega, the past no longer controls the present, while the future is infinite yet indefinite. Omega is a floating, buzzing, transitory state. Herein lies the source of both its strength and its fragility.

A company in Omega is vulnerable to the pushes and pulls of the needs of its constituents. Without order, those pushes and pulls can become self-serving and pitch the entity back into Gamma. Too many unrealized expectations in Omega can create a dangerous backlash. Too much unrestrained enthusiasm, and the baby can inadvertently be thrown out with the bathwater.

In the Omega state the revolutionary option and the new ideas that rise from the rubble of old barriers develop into a workable system. Since there tends to be more enthusiasm than wisdom in Omega, it is a time for caution. Discipline and order must resume if the positive energy of liberation is to be channeled productively.

A leader of a company in Omega must maintain a judicious balance between prudence and a readiness to respond. The wise leader takes slow, steady steps while remaining primed to quicken the pace when that is needed to ensure a solid, endurable entity. Given sufficient time, a well-managed company that has survived Gamma and found a future in Omega will mature into a new state of Alpha.

New Alpha, After Omega

New Alpha is the final consolidation of the ideas and coping systems that emerge during Omega. The corporation is once again in harmony with its environment, its market, its industry, and its constituents. Having reached a new plateau of productivity, it is ready to start over again.

Conclusion

In today's turbulent business environment, there are no hard-and-fast conclusions—only transitions. Those who truly comprehend the nature of turbulence recognize the futility of searching for rigid solutions. My goal in writing this book is to help you turn that understanding into new opportunities.

During my years in business, I have developed an empowering relationship with change rather than one that is adversarial. I have come to realize that steady-state existence is an illusion.

We live and do business in a world that is in a constant state of flux. We slip in and out of various turbulent states, seemingly without warning. The length of time spent in any given state is indeterminable, and the way to make a transition is murky at best.

If I have learned anything from my experiences leading, building, and rebuilding companies, it is that turbulence and a certain amount of chaos are inevitable. To manage such flux effectively, we must learn to be flexible and adapt to shifts that seem to become more profound as time goes on. In other words, we must be ready for anything!

Turbulence is neither negative nor positive: it is simply the constant advent of change. As you read this book, I hope you will come to appreciate that with danger and risk walk opportunity and reward. As we struggle to find order in an ever-changing world, the impact of turbulence on the environment in which we do business is inescapable. The question is, will you be ready?

2

Nobody Flies Solo: Building the Senior Management Team

If you are going to manage effectively through turbulence, it is essential to master the basics. As any stunt pilot knows, you can't "push the envelope" unless you follow the fundamental rules. You must never exceed the airplane's flying capabilities, design limits, and the maximum ranges of safety.

The first building block in creating or maintaining a company that can handle turbulence is strong, decisive leadership. That leadership must balance certain essential interlocking skills and values, or the entity will falter. In order to be effective, the top person in any company must, at one time or another, be able to wear the following ten hats:

1. Visionary
2. Role model
3. Empowerer
4. Facilitator
5. Cheerleader
6. Listener
7. Mentor-student
8. Friend

9. Disciplinarian

10. Spokesperson

I discuss each of these roles more fully later in this chapter, and you will learn more about how these attributes come into play in navigating the winds of turbulence. But first I'd like to tell you something about my approach to business.

I often describe my leadership style as being high-touch rather than high-tech. I find joy and courage in the team. I like working with people I can call my friends. For me, a positive experience is more enjoyable and a difficult one more endurable when others are involved. As a youngster growing up on a small family-run farm, I saw that the need for teamwork was critical. This value has been reinforced in every aspect of my life, but particularly in business.

I adapted this chapter title from a phrase my friend, mentor, and one-time boss liked to use. The late Eddie Carlson was the chairman at United Airlines. I can almost picture him saying, "Nobody sings solo." This expression referred to the interdependence we in the corporate world share with our customers, employees, suppliers, lenders, shareholders—even our competitors. I have Eddie to thank for teaching me the value of the team concept as it applies to running a company.

It's interesting that Eddie talked in terms of *singing* solo. As it happens, I have been singing ever since my boyhood. These days, I do most of my singing in the church choir. When I was in high school, I sang in the boys' quartet. The four of us—Edwin Stock, Bill Osborne, Roger Reith, and I—formed a musical team: Edwin sang first tenor; Bill sang second tenor; Roger sang bass; and I sang baritone.

We practiced and trained with our instructor almost every day. The four of us made appearances at school functions, church socials, civic events, and recitals, but the highlight of our time together was when we prepared for the district and state music contests.

As we learned about music and singing, we also learned a great deal about each other. The friendship and comradery between us grew strong. By the time we performed at our first district contest, we were a team in every sense of the word. As we stood on that stage, we all realized that none of us was strong enough individually to have accomplished this much on our own. The strength to sing our very best came from being part of a team.

Although none of us had the vocabulary to say it, I believe we all recognized that the whole was greater than the parts. There was added value in the togetherness we had achieved, and that is the essence of any team. For the most part, the four of us stuck together. I can, however, recall one notable exception.

As I was getting dressed on the morning of the district music contest, I remembered that we were all required to wear blue jackets and red ties. Unfortunately, none of my three ties was the right color. I went to my parents' bedroom, opened the door to my father's closet, and started searching for a red tie. There was only one red one in my father's closet—a deep, beautiful shade of red adorned with the hand-painted figure of a duck. I nervously removed it from the rack, tied a fast knot, and rushed outside to catch the school bus that would take me and the rest of the quartet to the town where the contest was being held. Because my parents were too busy running the station to come hear me sing, my father wouldn't find out that I had taken his tie without asking.

As it turned out, we won the contest. Looking back on it now, I can identify all the elements that make for a successful team. We had a firm yet friendly leader. We each had a voice of our own, but we had learned to use our individual skills as if we were singing with one voice. In retrospect, this team had the three key ingredients for success—leadership, balance, and a sense of purpose.

Like most teams after a win, we were jubilant. As we walked through town, Bill took a cigar out of his pocket. "Care to celebrate as gentlemen celebrate?" he asked.

The cigar was passed from one victor to the next, until it was in my hands. But before I was able to take my self-congratulatory puff, we spied a teacher coming our way. There was no inconspicuous place to throw or hide the cigar, and the teacher would catch me if I didn't think of something fast. I quickly cupped the cigar in my right hand and slipped it down the inside pocket of my sport coat, hoping to contain the cigar smoke.

The teacher walked by, barely giving us a nod, but I had another problem. Along with the cigar, I unwittingly had cupped my father's tie in my hand. As I pulled my hand out from within my jacket, the smell of burning fabric accompanied the whitish-blue wisps spiraling into the open air. I found a one-inch hole burned straight through the tailfeathers of the hand-painted duck. My teammates gave me a look that said unequivocally, "You're on your own, pal." I realized at that moment that there are times in life when we all do have to fly solo. The duck got his. Now I was going to get mine.

Teamwork and Teamthink

Much of the talk in recent years about teamwork and cooperation in corporate America is little more than lip service. Unfortunately, teamwork is not yet a broad-based reality because most CEOs and senior managers have not understood the benefits of empowerment, relinquishing power and control to teams and networks of people. In other instances, what looks like teamwork is nothing more than a group of people implementing the ideas or orders of a soloist CEO or chairperson. To take teamwork beyond this level requires creating what I call *teamthink* as a regular part of decision making and strategic planning.

It is almost impossible to discuss the benefits of corporate teamwork without at least mentioning Japanese business techniques. Because the Japanese have been so successful at fostering cooperation among their employees, many Americans feel it's logical for us to emulate their methods. I don't believe, however, that it is a productive approach for most American companies.

Japan is a homogeneous society. The Japanese have, essentially, one race, one culture, and one history, and the spirit of the team is a natural outgrowth of that culture. The United States, on the other hand, is, as it has always been, a heterogeneous society consisting of people with origins in diverse cultures around the world. Such diversity makes it difficult, if not impossible, to emulate Japanese-style teamwork. Our society stresses the rights, thoughts, and opinions of the individual. Japan is much more a country of conformists.

If we are going to instill *teamthink* into our businesses, we can't do it by copying Japanese management techniques. Homogene-

ous teams, such as those found in successful Japanese corporations, find strength in similarity. Heterogeneous teams, such as
those in America, draw strength from a fortuitous blend of interlocking individual talents.

Because our society is driven by the spirit of individual excellence, we must emphasize that quality when we build teams in
American corporations—especially the senior management teams
that must lead the company as a team into the new century. For
American business to be competitive, such teams must replace
the outdated mode of CEO or chairperson as solo leader.

My experience has shown that American teamwork can be
extraordinary. When I was at United, 50,000 people of diverse
backgrounds created the largest airline in the Western world.
When I was at Braniff, hundreds of employees successfully took
a major airline through a $1 billion restructuring so it could fly
again. When I was at Southwest, hundreds of people took a small
entrepreneurial airline and turned it into the most profitable carrier in the United States. To me, this is the essence of teamwork—
American style.

*   *   *

Over the years, the Dallas Salvation Army has benefited from
the direction provided by a wide variety of excellent civic and
business leaders—including Roger Staubach, Margo Perot, and
the late U.S. Representative Jim Collins. At one point, board chair
Ruth Sharp Altschuler asked if I would form an advisory council
for the Adult Rehabilitation Center, a $4 million arm of the
Dallas Salvation Army.

I agreed to take the assignment as a volunteer on two conditions: council members would be selected based on the skills and
the values they could bring to the organization; and the organization would operate like a for-profit business, even though profit
was not its primary goal.

Any organization through which $4 million flows annually,
whether profit or nonprofit, must have a balanced advisory board
as well as a competent senior management team. We needed a
leader, and I agreed to assume that responsibility. We also needed
volunteers to provide leadership in such areas as finance, accounting, marketing, and administration.

In coordination with Captain Bill Madison, the Salvation Army officer in charge of the Rehabilitation Center, we selected individuals with the necessary skills and values to meet the demands of the Rehabilitation Center and the mission of the Salvation Army. For our accounting and auditing needs, we selected the managing partner of a big eight accounting firm. For financial aspects, we chose the president of a bank. To oversee property acquisitions, property management, and leases, we chose a successful Dallas real estate developer.

We selected a prominent Dallas attorney to handle legal matters and the president of an advertising agency to oversee advertising, direct-mail campaigns, and public relations. The vice president of marketing for an airline brought his marketing skills to the council, and the president of the children's division of a large retail chain donated his expertise in the area of merchandising. A former president of the Dallas Junior League brought organizational and administrative skills into the mix. To complete the team, we added the senior vice presidents of the local electric and telephone companies.

The team council set up for the Adult Rehabilitation Center of the Dallas Salvation Army has been very successful. Programs run by the Adult Rehabilitation Center generate all the revenue necessary to operate the center, including several thrift shops that sell donated items. As a result, there has been no need to solicit cash contributions.

The process for building the team at the Salvation Army was similar to that of building the teams at Southwest and Braniff. The major difference came down to a question of timing. Each entity was at a very different stage in its development. The Salvation Army Adult Rehabilitation Center had existed for many years, but its advisory council was just forming; we created the team from a blank slate.

At Southwest, the company was young and growing fast. When I came to the airline, many of the senior people responsible for the company's success were already in place. My job was to evaluate the abilities of those individuals and observe their strengths and weaknesses. Only then could I determine the kind of people that were needed to complete the senior team. At Braniff, as at Southwest, many of the senior people were responsible for that company's poor state of health. I evaluated the team to determine who would stay and who would go. At Braniff, however, I worked without the luxury of time I was afforded at the Salvation Army and Southwest.

At the Salvation Army, our only prompt was how quickly we wanted to organize. If we chose to conduct a lengthy interview process and long deliberations over who was best for the various positions, we had the latitude to do so.

Although I didn't have unlimited time to build a senior management team at Southwest, I was able to operate within relatively comfortable parameters. The momentum of the organization carried it while I determined precisely who the airline needed to take it to its next phase. The talented people I chose had value systems that fit not only the existing corporate culture but also the mature culture that would develop as Southwest grew larger. A CEO cannot ask for a more rewarding task.

My experiences at Braniff, however, were a different story. Virtually everything vital to the company had to happen in two to three weeks, especially the formation of the senior management team. Some individuals had to go; some had to stay; and some had to be brought in to fill the holes. We had to be accurate in our choices because there are no second chances when you are faced with the kind of crisis Braniff was suffering.

We sought out survivors within the existing personnel. Who, we asked ourselves, would be able to play a role in turning the company around? We looked for men and women who were willing to take on additional responsibility and forge ahead. We tried to bring in people from outside the airline who would fit in with those who remained, while simultaneously adding a new perspective.

Each of these three entities—the Salvation Army, Southwest Airlines, and Braniff International—required a different kind of leadership team. But despite their differences, each entity needed a team built upon the same fundamental elements.

My years in business—from Capital, to United, to Southwest, to Braniff, to my continued involvement with the board of the Dallas Salvation Army, to the principles I use in running my own consulting and public speaking company—have taught me to recognize the elements that make a truly successful team. The ideal team in American corporations and organizations is not comprised of people who think and act the same but is a group of individuals with different talents who can work together effectively to achieve the three critical elements of teamthink—purpose, leadership, and balance.

Chapter 5 discusses the importance of defining a company's mission and purpose through the development of superordinate goals. For now, I explore the areas of leadership and balance.

Leadership

Leadership is the first essential building block in creating a strong senior management team—or, for that matter, any kind of successful team. Leadership occurs on many levels within a company, but the two most important levels are the leadership the CEO gives to the senior management team and the leadership that team imparts to everyone else in the company. Although the senior management team is responsible for a company's leadership, the CEO is accountable to the board, consumers, investors, analysts, employees, members of the senior team, the media, and the community. In assuming the role of leader, the CEO serves all these constituents. This is both the most confounding and most rewarding aspect of leadership.

One useful way to describe leadership is to list the diverse roles the leader must play. A good leader is a cheerleader when he or she needs to be and is equally competent when the time comes to be a disciplinarian. The best leaders can slip in and out of these roles naturally. This same flexibility is the basis for effective senior-body leadership.

Earlier in this chapter, I mentioned that there are ten hats that an effective leader must don at various times. I'd like you to consider each quality and how each relates to your particular strengths.

VISIONARY

A visionary is often characterized as a person with great dreams. A visionary business leader has such dreams about his or her business and where that business should be in relation to the unfolding future. The distinction between visionaries and dreamers is that visionaries assume the responsibility to create the future they see for their companies; dreamers do not.

Vision is a complex attribute. Within it are contained such intangibles as hope, faith, desire, ambition, and dreams—as well as the practical talents to bring these intangibles to fruition.

A visionary possesses imagination, creativity, and curiosity. Vision is the spark for the commitments and promises that construct the future. A visionary must have the courage to provide unwavering direction—the kind that fosters steady forward movement.

ROLE MODEL

As role model, the leader sets the primary example of the ethical standards of the organization. He or she represents the value system by which the company operates—as well as the cultural environment in which it conducts business.

The most subtle but enabling way to lead is not by direction but by example—by being a model for excellence, integrity, and compassion. A team cannot be expected to have values that contradict those of its leader.

EMPOWERER

A leader empowers members of the senior management team by giving them the responsibility to accomplish goals, the tools necessary to achieve such accomplishments, and accountability for the outcome. It takes considerable courage on the CEO's part to delegate authority freely and allow those to whom it has been granted to flourish.

FACILITATOR

When I was getting ready to move from United to Southwest, Eddie Carlson said, "Howard, remember, as CEO you never have a good idea. All the good ideas come from your senior management team, your directors, and your employees." In fulfilling the role of facilitator, a leader makes suggestions, plants seeds, gives encouragement, and nurtures new ideas that are generated by the group. The essence of a cooperative leadership style is a CEO's willingness to put his or her ego second to the desire to serve all constituents.

Many CEOs have yet to make this important shift in attitude. The CEO as leader of a company is actually its most humble servant. He or she is ultimately accountable to every employee, every customer, every supplier, every lender, and every share-holder—as well as to the chairperson, the board, and the public. In humble service, no leader may ask any member of the senior management team—or any member of the company—to perform a labor or task that he or she would not be ready and willing to perform should the need arise.

CHEERLEADER

A good leader has a smile even when a frown would be a more spontaneous response. The forward momentum of a team is the responsibility of the leader. It is his or her role to encourage, prompt, and challenge senior managers to do their absolute best. To wear this hat, a leader needs to develop both intimate and broad-based relationships. In addition to having a good one-to-one relationship with each member of the senior management team, a leader must establish and maintain a sweeping relation-ship with the entire company and the public at large.

LISTENER

Every CEO I have ever met has had two ears and one mouth. Effective leaders employ those organs in that ratio. Listening should be active: that means paying careful attention to the speaker's suggestions, comments, problems, complaints, and praises.

Active listening requires empathy, understanding, tolerance, compassion, gratitude—whatever response is appropriate for the message. Passive listening is merely an obligatory registration of the sounds of words, a kind of listening that does little for the speaker and even less for the leader on the receiving end.

Good communication always begins with active listening. This is the only way to create trust and provide a secure setting for meaningful exchanges in the future. A quick rule of thumb can help you evaluate yourself and others in this aspect of leadership: if your (or someone else's) speaking takes up more than half of the time you devote to communicating, something is wrong!

MENTOR AND STUDENT

Most leaders have a great deal to offer. If you are in a leadership position, you probably have had many years of business and personal experience. My advice to leaders is to impart their knowledge and wisdom to others in useful and empowering ways. The best leaders use their knowledge and experience to guide and support those they lead. They have a genuine desire to help their people grow and mature into leaders themselves.

Contrary to popular belief, knowledge by itself is not power. Power can be galvanized only through the organized and purposeful use of knowledge. In the process of mentoring those we lead, we must remember how we acquired the knowledge, experience, and wisdom we are now able to impart.

At one time or another, everyone has had a mentor. Those of us who truly understand the value of such relationships maintain them throughout our lives. This involves recognizing that we are always students. I believe that we can always learn something from everyone with whom we interact. An individual's experiences create a unique pool of knowledge not held in the same quality or quantity by anyone else. That means each person has something singular to share.

In addition to listening actively, one should also learn actively. Do not simply wait to be taught or for information to come your way. Take information from others by actively soliciting their knowledge.

As a student, a true leader makes mistakes and admits them. He or she then corrects the mistakes and moves on. Like any discipline, leadership takes practice. When we practice, it is only natural to make mistakes. A mistake is a wonderful way to learn. Without mistakes, none of us would ever learn enough to become mentors!

FRIEND

Many leaders will tell you that friendship is not a prerequisite for leadership. Perhaps they are right. I believe, however, that friendship and friendliness are prerequisites for the strongest kind of leadership.

One-to-one relationships between the leader of the senior management team and other senior managers make for enabling and enjoyable interaction. This is the most fertile atmosphere for creating a productive business environment.

Friendly leadership dispenses with formality and ostentation. It fosters the communication, discourse, and interchanges that often lead to personal friendship between a leader and other team members.

Friendship between leader and those being led is not a sign of weakness in a team; it is a sign of strength. It takes a strong and courageous leader to win both the respect and the friendship of other team members. In times of crisis, the friendship between individuals sometimes creates the cohesiveness that ultimately carries them through.

DISCIPLINARIAN

Conflict in an organization is inevitable. Although parenting employees is inappropriate, dispensing discipline of one kind or another is often necessary. A disciplinarian is generally thought of as someone who brings order. I use the term in a twofold manner: one who disciplines and one who possesses discipline.

A leader who disciplines must embody justice and fairness. He or she must resolve, personally if necessary, conflicts that arise within the senior management team or elsewhere in the company. A CEO should not intentionally supplant the authority of other managers in the company, but he or she must always put the welfare of the company ahead of protocol and delicate egos.

The other kind of disciplinarian is the leader who has self-discipline. By that, I mean a CEO who by example exercises self-control and takes the lead in setting high standards of behavior. In my view, one of the most essential responsibilities of a company leader is to maintain the values to which others are expected to adhere.

Discipline may mean arriving for work early or leaving late. It may mean abstaining from the use of alcohol at company functions. It may mean maintaining a trim and healthy appearance through regular exercise or dressing as you would like others in the company to dress. Discipline may require that a leader use appropriate language—both grammatically and in terms of content—with all constituents.

Discipline in this sense refers not to the administration of justice, but to the practice of customs, behaviors, and values the CEO feels are necessary to help move the company toward its goals. There is, in fact, more than a semantic relationship between the two concepts of discipline. When a high standard of behavior is scrupulously maintained by a company's leaders, the potential for conflict and the need to reprimand are always reduced.

SPOKESPERSON

If you want to be an effective leader, don't hide from your company or from the public—particularly during times of trouble. As spokesperson, the CEO's statements should have constancy, consistency, and continuity. Make statements to constituents at regular intervals. They should be uniform, not contradictory, from one moment to the next. Statements should flow logically; they should be reflections of what is really happening within the company, not a facade.

The leader as spokesperson symbolizes the entire company. In good economic times, constituents look to the CEO for inspiration and recognition. In times of economic difficulty, constituents look for confidence and encouragement. In donning the spokesperson's hat, the CEO assumes the responsibility for satisfying those needs.

In favorable and profitable times, the CEO-as-spokesperson gives credit where credit is due. In difficult or critical times, spokespersons accept responsibility and accountability for the situation. Here is yet one more example of the difficult but rewarding paradox of leadership.

*   *   *

The most effective leaders possess a combination of the ten attributes discussed in this section. Together, these qualities give the CEO, or any leader within the company, the voice of authority—a voice he or she should rarely have to raise. In finding a single concept to describe a CEO, I would like to redefine those letters to mean *chief empowerment officer.* Empowerment, in my view, is the CEO's true test of leadership, while service is his or her ultimate responsibility.

Balance

Balance is the second fundamental component of the senior management team. It is the equilibrium between the skills and the values of the members.

I like to compare the basic set of abilities needed by each member of the senior management team to a skill tree. As a company grows, so must an individual leader's skills. New branches represent new expertise, and branches that reach higher represent advanced levels of an existing skill. As the skills of a company's leaders continue to flourish, the growth of that entity is enhanced.

This symbiotic relationship sometimes can put a company into a Catch-22 situation. If the individuals within a company do not grow, neither will the company. Likewise, if a company stagnates, the individuals within it also will stagnate.

Occasionally, a company and its people plateau: they no longer advance each other. When this occurs, it is time to force-feed new skills. Sometimes a company implements this through retraining or advanced education. More often, the board force-feeds new skills by bringing in new personnel with new abilities and ideas.

My experiences at Southwest and Braniff illustrate this issue. In order to grow, both airlines needed an infusion of new skills. Southwest wanted to become a full-fledged, highly competitive regional carrier; Braniff needed financial stability and direction.

The boards of each of these companies looked outside for solutions.

Once a company crosses a plateau or breaks through a *skills obstacle,* the company and its members, from senior level to front line, co-nurture one another. At Southwest, we tripled profits in three years. At Braniff, we reorganized in record time and started flying again. In both cases, we were able to accomplish our goals by utilizing appropriate skills and values.

The following list of skills is by no means exhaustive. It does not include all the abilities displayed by effective participants in the senior management team, but it does cover the general aptitudes and qualities each member of the team should possess.

UNDERSTAND AND ASSUME A POSITIVE ROLE IN THE DYNAMICS OF YOUR TEAM

A team experiences a definite psychology and set of dynamics. Most individuals who have been part of any successful team understand this. There is an evolutionary process that begins with most members experiencing some uneasiness about other members. This is due almost entirely to a lack of familiarity among the members. Given time for the participants to develop a foundation of shared experience, this sense of uneasiness is often replaced by feelings of comradeship, trust, and mutual dependency.

If there are strong feelings of uneasiness between team members—for any reason save a breach of ethics—each participant has to exercise tolerance and patience. In time, understanding and mutual acceptance will open the door to a state of harmony.

It is important for senior managers to understand that within the team dynamic, the CEO-as-leader has the most difficult role. The person who heads the team must earn the respect, loyalty, and, one hopes, the friendship of all team members before a harmonious state can be achieved.

Although the CEO should not try to dominate the group, he or she has to maintain a position of strength relative to the other team members. The leader must always have the final say in any situation where it is warranted—while, at the same time, making it clear that he or she is there to render service to both the team and the company.

The goal of the team is to create a highly productive and harmonious organism with just enough anarchy from its members and direction from the CEO to maintain an evolutionary—and sometimes revolutionary—process.

MANAGE WITH DEDICATION, BUT DON'T LET STRESS UNDERMINE YOUR PHYSICAL AND MENTAL HEALTH

Every phase of a business, from start-up to turnaround, requires dedication. Nowhere is this more true than with the senior management team.

Senior managers must be able to put in long hours without risking their health or the welfare of their families. They must meet the demands of the position but not at the price of sacrificing balanced and enjoyable lives. Because of the level of responsibility and accountability placed upon them, senior managers operate under high pressure. It's essential that they learn to manipulate stress to their benefit.

To meet the challenge of leadership, the frustrations and negative energies generated by the realities of doing business need to be transformed into constructive energies. There are any number of ways to accomplish this. Some people use exercise to alleviate stress and negative energy; some use relaxation techniques. Some men and women find relief through spiritual outlets, while others practice various kinds of meditation. Use whatever is right for you, but please don't allow stress to cause a potentially fatal imbalance in your life.

ENCOURAGE YOUR PEOPLE TO THINK AND ACT INDEPENDENTLY

At first, independence may seem incompatible with the team concept. Nothing could be further from the truth. The most effective teams consist of strong, independent members who can apply their skills collectively.

Picture a tree that is majestic in appearance and healthy at its core. Such a tree is not sustained by one large root but has many strong, independent roots that work together to support and nourish it. In business as in nature, balance is essential. To lead effectively, senior managers must strike an equilibrium between individual initiative and commitment to the team.

MAINTAIN A VISION OF YOUR LONG-TERM OBJECTIVES WHILE RETAINING THE ABILITY TO ACT QUICKLY

This statement encompasses two essential but somewhat polarized skills. On the one hand, a company's leader must be able to take the long view—never losing sight of the big picture. He or she must be able to create and implement plans that yield long-term results. On the other hand, that leader must be willing and able to do whatever it takes on a day-to-day basis to remove an obstacle or move a particular situation forward.

A good leader must possess a balance of skills to address long- and short-term needs, particularly when a company is experiencing turbulence. Your ability to make fast but appropriate decisions can be called upon at any moment. At the same time, you must never do anything without considering its ultimate effect on the long-term welfare of your company.

OBTAIN BASIC TECHNICAL AND EDUCATIONAL SKILLS COMMENSURATE WITH YOUR RESPONSIBILITIES. BE READY AND WILLING TO ACQUIRE NEW SKILLS AND EDUCATION WHEN NECESSARY

Although every senior manager and CEO is stronger in some areas than in others, he or she should have a working knowledge of all major aspects of the company. In addition to an appropriate educational background and relevant business experience, the manager should be ready to learn whatever new information and techniques are needed to provide effective leadership.

Like all men and women who must juggle complex tasks, business leaders never outgrow the need for training, retraining, and advanced training. Without new input, we become stagnant and lose the edge we need to navigate the winds of turbulence.

BE ABLE TO ACCEPT NEGATIVE CRITICISM WHILE MAINTAINING A HEALTHY EGO

The greater an individual's responsibilities, the more praise and criticism that individual receives. For most of us, praise is far easier to accept than criticism of any kind. Nevertheless, most successful people have learned to appreciate the benefits of constructive criticism—particularly when it comes from people we believe to be on our side.

Part of the price you pay for assuming leadership is the dubious honor of receiving beefs and gripes from all directions: your employees, customers, the public, the media, and the board. This is particularly true when a company is experiencing tough times. In many instances, such negative criticism contains grains of truth that can be useful. Unfortunately, these potentially valuable nuggets are often shrouded in emotions such as anger, frustration, disappointment—even jealousy.

As someone who has suffered his share of negative criticism, I have found that the wisest course is to separate the emotion and try to discern whether there is anything valid to be learned. Leading a company is not a job for the thin-skinned. No matter how strong the team, the spotlight of criticism will always focus most brightly on the person in charge—particularly when the going gets tough.

I have seen highly skilled men and women fold up their tents under this kind of pressure. The ones who can outlast the winds of turbulence are those with the ego strength to use negative criticism the same way they use positive feedback—as opportunities for self-improvement.

Conclusion

Leadership is a balancing act requiring several important ingredients and values outlined earlier. I believe leadership will be the key ingredient in an organization's stability and success in the 1990s. Courage and stamina will be required to develop and work with a team of employees and managers. They must be empowered with accountability and with the authority to accomplish tasks without the old ways of bureaucratic control. Remember, "Nobody flies solo" for very long successfully.

3

What's in It for Me?
Fulfilling Employee
Dreams

We all have dreams of one kind or another. Some of us dream of riches, mansions, and antique cars. Some dream of tropical islands, blue water, white sand, and ocean wind. Some dream of quiet, relaxing times shared with family and friends. For the most part, such dreams are not about working—except perhaps a burning desire to stop. One study cited in *Newsweek* concluded that the average American would not work if he or she did not need to do so to survive. That same study found that the average Japanese man or woman would continue working even if economic need was no longer a factor.

Although many Americans may dream of early retirement, the vast majority of millionaires in this country work. I am reminded of a security guard named Curtis Sharp who won several million dollars in the New York State lottery. Several weeks after reality set in, a reporter asked Sharp what he was going to do now that he was a rich man. "I'm going right back to work," he replied. "I've got to get away from all this money."

Most of us will never have the luxury of being able to choose whether or not we want to work. Since we appear destined to spend a significant portion of our time in the workplace, we had better try to satisfy at least some of our dreams there. We can only realistically expect the workplace to satisfy the needs and wants created within its own context. Still, to the extent that we envision an ideal work experience—or at least one that is positive—there are ways to fulfill that dream.

Back in the early 1960s when companies still used keypunch machines to assist computers in processing information, I met a woman named Mary who operated one of those big, loud, monotonous devices. She worked eight hours a day in a lonely, windowless room for minimum wage. When I asked Mary how she stood the drudgery of creating keypunch cards all day, I expected her to say that this was something she needed to do for the money. I received an answer that surprised me. She told me that she loved her work. She certainly did not want to keypunch all day, but she found it easy to get out of bed each morning and keep a smile on her face throughout the day because she felt that she was helping others do their jobs. Mary had found a sense of purpose in her work, and that kept her motivated and happy.

As the years have passed, I haven't come across too many people like Mary. Most of us are motivated by more basic needs, such as the need to pay the bills, to affiliate, to enjoy what we are doing, to receive recognition, to face a challenge, and to achieve. Rarely are we driven by the satisfaction that comes from serving others.

I have often thought about this exceptional woman. I knew nothing of her background, but I wondered whether she was wealthy, so that a steady paycheck had no importance to her. Perhaps she had a close family or network of friends, so the need to belong was not a priority. What's important about Mary's story is that her employer made it possible for her to find purpose in what she did.

This is the key to need satisfaction for employees: provide the *possibility* for satisfaction and offer employees the opportunity to seize that possibility. Not all needs can be satisfied by the workplace, nor should they be. Not all individuals have the same set of needs to be filled in the same order. But since work is such an important part of life, many needs can and should be at least partially fulfilled through the workplace. The question is, which needs should a company try to address?

THE NEEDS HIERARCHY

Transcendent Needs

LEVEL 5

(Purpose)   (Significance)   (Love)

Complex Individual Needs

LEVEL 4

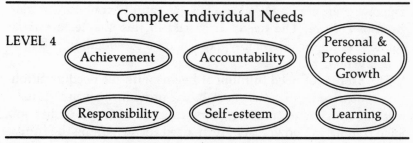

(Achievement)   (Accountability)   (Personal & Professional Growth)

(Responsibility)   (Self-esteem)   (Learning)

Simple Individual Needs

LEVEL 3

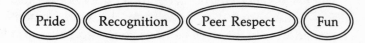

(Pride)(Recognition)(Peer Respect)(Fun)

Environment Needs

LEVEL 2

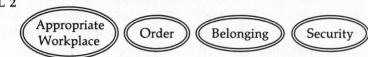

(Appropriate Workplace)(Order)(Belonging)(Security)

Basic Needs

LEVEL 1

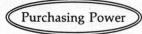

(Purchasing Power)

Based in part on Abraham H. Maslow's "humanistic psychology" approach to needs satisfaction.

The Needs Hierarchy

Certain basic wants and needs must be fulfilled before employees can be productive and harmonious within their environment. In general, the needs a company can potentially satisfy are those created by the work experience and those that overlap with other aspects of an employee's life, such as family, community, religion, or culture. The needs discussed in this chapter are those employees might reasonably expect to be provided, in full or in part, by their jobs.

The process of need fulfillment begins with the need traditionally considered to be the most basic: providing an individual a level of purchasing power commensurate with his or her job. Such purchasing power is, in turn, used for sustaining the fundamental needs of food and shelter. Once basic needs are satisfied, we proceed to more subtle and complex motivations.

The needs hierarchy model on p. 41 does not try to address all needs—only those that flow from the work experience. The model addresses the needs I have found to be most relevant to employees. In general, the needs that are lower in the hierarchy must be addressed first. As each level of needs is fulfilled, increased productivity results, and a new level of needs is created.

As you read, try to place yourself inside the model. Think about how motivated and productive you might be if, for example, you were not paid a reasonable wage for your work. Consider how you might perform in an environment that was not conducive to fulfilling your responsibilities.

How productive would you be, for example, if your office temperature was 92 degrees and you had no desk or chair? What if, on the other hand, your office was 72 degrees with a large desk, comfortable chair, telephone, and water fountain? Consider how your productivity might further increase if you enjoyed what you did, if you learned as you worked, if you received recognition for your achievements, and, ultimately, if you found significance in your work.

The needs hierarchy is a living model. It is highly flexible: its circles can shrink or enlarge; as the model evolves, other needs can be placed between those that already exist. Rather than thinking of the model as a series of patterns to which you must conform, use it to respond to the kinds of changing needs that are particularly volatile during turbulent times.

LEVEL 1: BASIC NEEDS

- Purchasing power

The most basic need an employee must have filled by an employer is some level of purchasing power commensurate with the task performed. An hourly wage or annual salary is the most common form of compensation. Supplementing this are bonuses, commissions, as well as profit-sharing and ownership plans.

At Southwest, our ownership and profit-sharing plans stated that shareholders would receive a return for their investment before any officer or employee profited. Once those outside stockholders were taken care of, employees were entitled to 15 percent of the remaining corporate profits for that calendar year, the maximum allowed by the IRS at that time.

Profits were divided based upon salary. An employee whose salary was 0.1 percent of the company's total salary expense was awarded 0.1 percent of the profits. If an employee's salary was 1 percent of the total salary expense, he or she received 1 percent of the profits—and so on. Employees became eligible for the program after one year with the company.

The mechanics of the system worked like this. Everybody from the president to people on the front line received a modest cash payment of $175 quarterly. At the end of the year, whatever cash was left from the percentage allocation was used to purchase Southwest stock on the New York Stock Exchange and credited to a designated account. The stock was purchased throughout the year by a trustee bank. We estimated annual earnings and made an aggregate profit-sharing payment to the trustee, usually on a quarterly basis. In turn, the trustee bought stock on the open market—we never knew when—and then credited it to the employees' accounts. A name was not attached to the shares in an account until the employee cashed in.

The plan was designed to fully vest over a minimum period of ten years. If you left before spending five years with the company, everything in your name was forfeited. Those monies were then returned to the fund to be shared by everyone. When I left after three years with Southwest to join Braniff, everything that had accumulated in my name went back into the system. One employee shook my hand on the day I left and said, jokingly, "You know, I'm sad to see you go. On the other hand, we all appreciate your forfeiture into the profit-sharing plan."

Previously, the plan had been changed to put 50 percent of an employee's allocation into stock and the remaining 50 percent into various fixed- and variable-income plans that the employee could choose. This allowed the employee to be involved in the program and ensured that an employee wouldn't lose everything if the stock market crashed. Incidentally, there was no pension fund at Southwest. All future income was derived from participation in the profit-sharing plan.

LEVEL 2: ENVIRONMENT NEEDS

- Appropriate workplace
- Order
- Belonging
- Security

The environment in which an employee works has a tremendous impact on productivity and happiness. Imagine an auto worker asked to assemble vehicles on an oil rig in the Pacific instead of in an appropriately designed factory. Imagine an executive asked to provide input on the company's strategic plan in an airplane-testing wind tunnel instead of in a conference room. Imagine an editor at a New York publishing house asked to do her job at the corner of Park Avenue and 44th Street, without a chair or telephone.

Employees need an appropriate workspace to do their jobs. This means providing a safe, comfortable, and stimulating setting—one that facilitates timely and competent completion of required tasks. People need the security of having a home base from which to operate—whether it's a desk and chair for an office worker, a car for a salesperson on the road, or a locker for a worker in a factory.

Beyond the physical environment, emotional and psychological needs must be satisfied. Most people need a sense of order and belonging. Order in the workplace is provided by creating sound policies and procedures and carrying them out in a rational and ethical manner. Most of us need to feel that what we do is both rational and ethical. A company's leaders are responsible for ensuring that those needs can be met within the work experience.

Order also grows out of scheduling time reasonably and flexibly. Management must never forget that all employees have lives outside the workplace. Many are wives and husbands, mothers and fathers. They may also be baseball coaches, PTA members, ministers, grandparents, or city council members.

Flexible scheduling will play an increasingly important role in the years to come. The four/ten (four days, ten hours a day) work week has been in effect for some time now. But in recent years, progressive companies have become much more innovative in their flextime scheduling. In the airline business, some companies have been successful with what is called the buddy system—a plan that allows two part-time employees to share a monthly flight schedule. They adjust the hours and days between them so that all professional and personal responsibilities can be fulfilled.

This system is particularly effective for single mothers and fathers and those with shared parenting responsibilities. Such highly flexible arrangements allow experienced and trained employees who might otherwise have to quit their jobs to continue working. The result is a win-win situation for all concerned: the company retains its investment in training and development, and the employee retains his or her job.

As we move into the twenty-first century, the labor force will continue to change. There will be many more older workers and a greater percentage of working women. Such changes require companies to respond appropriately.

I feel strongly that there should be no mandatory age at which talented people are forced to retire. More often than not, an older individual's family responsibilities are not as pressing as they once were, which leaves the person with far more time and energy to devote to work. Why not let such capable older men and women exercise that option?

By the year 2000 women will comprise more than 50 percent

of the nation's workers. That means companies are going to have to become more involved in creating and implementing workable child-care programs.

As more mothers of young children enter the workplace and more fathers take an increasingly active role in child rearing, companies need to be innovative in coming up with appropriate and flexible solutions. A particularly successful flextime system has been set up in Dallas by Baylor Hospital. It is called the two-day alternative. Baylor had difficulty getting nurses to work on weekends, so it created a work schedule that allowed most nurses to take weekends off. To compensate, they designed two twelve-hour shifts—one on Saturday and one on Sunday—for nurses who wanted to work only twenty-four hours but get paid for forty hours. This system satisfied the needs of both the nurses and the hospital.

Beyond the need for order, most employees have a strong need to feel that they belong—that they are part of a team. Like so many other things, this esprit de corps starts with the CEO.

At Southwest, senior management arrived on the job between 7:30 A.M. and 8:00 A.M. and was always visible. My personal routine was to arrive about 7:15 A.M., plunk everything down on my desk, and walk to the flight operations area—the place where pilots and flight attendants gathered as they checked in for the day. This regimen gave me a head start on the day's operations and gave employees an understanding of my commitment to them. Both they and I benefited by this ongoing personal and professional interaction.

Since the airline industry is a real-time business, one must look at what is happening hourly—not weekly or monthly. The commitment of the senior management team was a living model of what was expected from employees. It was leadership by example, still the best kind around. All members of the senior management team made many trips around the operation throughout the day to communicate or simply to be there. This is where the esprit de corps begins. As a leader, it is up to you to build upon it.

Finally, a sense of security is an important level 2 environmental need—from the point of view of safety as well as dependability, stability, and loyalty. Security is the sense that a company and an employee's job are going to continue to be there. Once again, a well-designed profit-sharing program helps create this sense of security and of building toward the future. Security is the unwritten assurance that if individuals maintain a sufficiently high quality of work to contribute to the profit plan, they will be around long enough to reap the fruit of their efforts.

A sense of security is created by the kind of operation a company's leaders run. Is it financially stable? Does it have a low turnover of personnel? When these questions can be answered affirmatively, employees have a sense of comfort about their companies and their jobs.

In general, companies with programs that create a safe and supportive environment for their employees are going to be desirable places to work. Companies that are responsive to employee needs both in and outside of the workplace attract the best people. Consequently, these companies will be the most competitive and most prepared to survive turbulence in the marketplace.

LEVEL 3: SIMPLE INDIVIDUAL NEEDS

- Pride
- Recognition
- Peer respect
- Fun

Because some of the needs on this level are covered in detail in other parts of the book, I will be brief in my discussion of them here. Basic and environment-level needs are sufficiently fundamental to be viewed as the foundation for the employee's work experience. Level 3 needs become important only after the needs on the two lower levels have been satisfied. Beyond these two levels, the order in which the needs must be satisfied tends to vary from person to person.

The needs in this section are simple because they are relatively easy to provide. Although an atmosphere of fun is easiest to implement when it is generated spontaneously from the CEO outward to the front line, it can be woven into the fabric of the company in systematic ways. Pride of accomplishment, recognition, and, to a certain extent, peer respect can also be provided systematically, particularly through an awards program.

In some cases, individuals have a greater need to learn than to enjoy themselves, which is one reason that the order of needs becomes more variable as we move into the next two levels of the hierarchy. A person may understand that he or she is not going to have fun every single day or every single moment on the job, but almost all employees have an underlying need to enjoy their work. I will have more to say about the need for fun in Chapter 7.

Once simpler personal needs have been satisfied, a person tends to become increasingly aware of deeper and more complex needs. This is why a company that wants to keep its employees happy and productive must also be willing to address the needs that are revealed at levels 4 and 5.

LEVEL 4: COMPLEX INDIVIDUAL NEEDS

- Achievement
- Responsibility
- Accountability
- Self-esteem
- Personal and professional growth
- Learning

The external, simple individual needs addressed at level 3 can go a long way in motivating individuals, but the most effective motivation always comes from within. Such intrinsic motivators as self-respect and self-esteem are more complicated and therefore harder to satisfy than the needs met at levels 1, 2, and 3.

One of the most effective ways to address complex individual needs is to give people the opportunity to meet a challenge successfully and then to reward them accordingly. Employees who have the desire to achieve must be given the opportunity to do so. In the old days, the reward usually given for achievement was a promotion. As more companies trim down their organizational structures, however, fewer promotions will be available for this purpose.

Superior achievement can be acknowledged by written and verbal communication, advanced training sessions, and formal awards. Leaders who keep their employees challenged encourage them to become involved in the experience of the company. Better still, they give employees the opportunity and incentive to help create what is going on.

At Southwest, we recognized that our flat organization limited opportunities for employees' upward movement. To compensate, we attempted to satisfy our employees' need to grow by providing lateral movement. Someone looking for or deserving a new experience or a challenge was offered the chance to either take a similar position in a new location or move to a job of equal importance and comparable salary but with different responsibilities. Our employees were able to grow through meeting these new challenges.

When a pond turns stagnant, it loses its vitality. The same principle applies to human beings. Although a flat organization cannot offer the same kinds of upward mobility as those with hierarchical structures, it can offer increased responsibility and accountability. For people who have had most of their needs satisfied on the lower levels of the hierarchy, these two elements can go a long way toward reinforcing feelings of self-esteem. "If my company thinks enough of me to expand my responsibilities and accountability," the individual reasons, "I must have value."

One effective way to satisfy the need for responsibility and accountability is by using deadlines. Timing is an important element of nearly every industry: reports need to be completed on time so they can be useful; airplanes need to get off the ground on time or an airport's entire operation will be jeopardized; broadcasts need to hit the airwaves on time so they don't back up other programs. Although timing is always an important business factor, using deadlines does not seem to be a priority in many companies. This kind of lax attitude can generate uncontrollable levels of turbulence. Consider for a moment the three major advantages of deadlines as a motivating force:

- Deadlines create urgency.
- Deadlines strip the "makework" from tasks and projects.

• Deadlines force people to be responsible and accountable, thus increasing productivity.

Deadlines should challenge your people without overwhelming them. The objective is to motivate employees to feel better about themselves by achieving more. When people are loaded down with more than they can handle, they can become frustrated and inefficient.

As a company attempts to satisfy more complex needs for its employees, the challenge to succeed becomes greater for all concerned. Giving responsibility to employees and making them accountable are important—both for the company as well as the individuals. Need satisfaction is really a two-way street; an employee needs responsibility and accountability to foster and maintain his or her sense of worth and value; at the same time, a company needs people who are motivated to take on more responsibility and accountability.

On this level of the hierarchy, some employees also have a need to learn and to grow. In many cases, these needs can be satisfied by providing on-the-job challenges. In other cases, a company must satisfy this need by giving the employee an experience outside the workplace.

In 1978 United sent me to the Advanced Management Program at Harvard University. For thirteen weeks I lived and studied with 160 other executives from companies around the world. We analyzed 220 case studies of corporations that had experienced unique situations in finance, marketing, or human relations. Through this experience I was able to learn about the challenges, successes, and failures of other companies in a formal classroom setting in a relatively short time. Perhaps even more important, I was also able to exchange ideas in an informal, friendly manner with the leaders of many companies. Some of these colleagues have since become valued friends and business associates.

The program also provided me with extended time away from business at United, which gave me a rare opportunity to reflect on the kind of challenges I was looking for in the future.

My goal for many years had been to become the CEO of an airline. Since Dick Ferris, United's CEO, was only a year or two older than I, the opportunities at that airline were slim to none.

I wasn't the type who could sit in the number two or three seat for many years waiting for the number one slot to become available.

I also was tired of the bureaucracy at United—the endless meetings and politics that interfere with progress in most very large organizations. At a company with a lean organizational structure I felt that I could build a results-oriented team. When I told my wife, Krista, that I wanted to leave United to run my own show, I had no idea where I would land, but spending thirteen weeks in academia recharged my mental batteries. The experience allowed me to stand back and take stock of myself. By the end of those thirteen weeks, I felt ready to make my move—if the right opportunity presented itself.

While I was at Harvard, I read that Lamar Muse, the CEO of Southwest Airlines in Dallas, had been fired. Whenever possible, I answer my own phone. The morning I arrived at my office in Chicago fresh from thirteen weeks at Harvard, the first phone call I answered was from Walter Haislip, an executive recruiter with a firm based in Dallas. "You are being considered as a candidate for the CEO position at Southwest Airlines," he said. "Would you meet with me if I flew to Chicago?"

After a series of meetings, I accepted the job. Apparently my participation in the Harvard program was not a factor in my selection as Southwest's CEO. Nevertheless, the two will forever be linked in my mind. Was it really a complete coincidence that the moment my vision of the future came clearly into focus, the exact opportunity I was looking for presented itself?

As you might imagine, I was not the only one pondering this question. Dick Ferris, United's CEO and the man who suggested that I participate in the Harvard program to enhance my value to the company, was livid to learn about my imminent departure. But Eddie Carlson, United's chairperson, recognized that when you allow people to expand their personal and professional horizons, you risk losing them.

I'll never forget how Eddie responded when Dick told him that I was leaving United. Eddie Carlson smiled, looked up at me through his glasses and asked, "Where are you going, Howard?"

"To Southwest Airlines in Dallas, Eddie," I replied. "I've been asked to come on board as president and CEO."

Eddie put his arm around me and said, "Howard, I think that is marvelous. I remember when I got my first CEO assignment and how thrilled I was." He turned to Dick: "You know, Dick, I was beginning to think we didn't have anyone good enough at United that anyone else wanted."

In the long run, a company only benefits from providing education and training for its people on all levels.

As we approach the twenty-first century, it is going to become increasingly important to have well-educated employees. Companies are going to be called upon to work closely with the schools to supplement an employee's education and eventually provide opportunities to further it. Because of the increasing multinationality of personnel in companies across the United States and the increasing amount of business we do abroad, forward-looking companies will want to help their employees learn more about the language and cultural protocol of their international customers.

LEVEL 5: TRANSCENDENT NEEDS

- Purpose
- Significance
- Love

At the beginning of this chapter, I spoke of Mary, a keypunch operator who loved her work. Mary was not keypunching because she was earning a good salary or because her need for fun or human contact were being satisfied. She was motivated only by the sense that she was needed and the simple desire to serve others. This woman's attitude demonstrates how a sense of purpose can make any job bearable—even enjoyable and worthwhile. Purpose is a difficult thing to instill in an individual from the outside. However, companies can do certain things to help people discover it on their own.

Sometimes the purpose of the individual matches the superordinate goal of the company; sometimes it is broader and deeper in scope than the underlying objectives of the company. In either case, once all other needs are satisfied, many employees need an internal rationale for doing what they are doing: they need a cause or a purpose. The easiest way to provide this is to encourage the individual to accept and support the superordinate goal of the company.

At Southwest, just after deregulation, we were going to begin interstate service to Louisiana from Love Field in Dallas. The cities of Dallas and Forth Worth tried to convince the Civil Aeronautics Board to restrict or prohibit Southwest from offering the service because they wanted the entire lucrative interstate operation to remain at the new Dallas-Fort Worth airport in which they had invested so much.

At that juncture, we thought it was important to ask the public for its opinion on the issue. We printed petitions and put them on all our flights and ticket counters; they were signed by our employees, passengers, and anyone else interested. Employees passed out the petitions on airplanes and traveled to downtown Dallas and Fort Worth, in uniform, to petition for signatures on street corners. Within one week, we collected over 70,000 signatures.

We made forty sets of copies of the signatures, creating 3,000 pounds of paper, which we then flew to Washington and delivered by moving van to the Civil Aeronautics Board. The message to the board was that the public wanted low-fare transportation from Love Field in Dallas to New Orleans.

When Congressman Jim Wright tried to put a rider on a bill in Congress that would give Dallas and Fort Worth the authority to restrict interstate service from Love Field, it was time for us to turn to the public again. This time, Southwest ran full-page ads in the newspaper with coupons. We asked supporters to fill out the coupons and send them to Senators Tower and Bentsen to make clear that the public wanted low-fare service to New Orleans from Love Field in Dallas. We delivered 60,000 coupons in multiple copies to Washington, negotiations began, and the Love Field Wright Amendment was drafted to allow Southwest to fly to any state contiguous to Texas. We felt that this was a compromise and that, in many respects, we had lost the battle. We wanted to fly to any state that made sense for the airline—not only those contiguous to Texas. Ultimately, Southwest was restricted to flying to contiguous states only out of Love Field, but we had the same freedom as other airlines to fly to cities in noncontiguous states from airports based in Houston.

Because no major airline wanted to move its operation to Love

Field and thereby restrict its flights to states that bordered Texas, the Wright Amendment ultimately turned into an opportunity. It allowed Southwest to own that niche in the market.

At 2:00 P.M. on a Friday we were granted our request for interstate service between Texas and Louisiana. In a display of flexibility and agility, we launched our inaugural flight that Friday night at 8:00 P.M. I was proud to take that flight along with nearly a full planeload of passengers.

In one way or another, almost every employee at Southwest contributed to helping us overcome this hurdle. The sense of purpose among people connected with the airline was at an all-time high. Everyone took pride in knowing that they had played a significant part in strengthening the company.

Nevertheless, complex needs such as purpose can never be completely satisfied by the workplace. A company's leaders must encourage employees to look outside the work experience for these satisfactions. One way to do this is to create fulfilling and meaningful experiences outside the company for employees.

One of the best places for an individual to turn to make a significant contribution is the community. Giving back something to the community deserves to be high on every corporation's agenda. Companies need to lead the way in volunteerism and working with nonprofit organizations within the communities in which they do business.

Senior management's responsibility is to set an example that encourages and supports employee involvement in such causes. I know of several corporations that allow selected employees to use their professional skills at various charitable organizations one day a month at company expense.

When an employee accomplishes something significant on behalf of the company or community, he or she needs to receive feedback and recognition. Eddie Carlson, former chairman at United, was famous for carrying in his suit pocket a leather recipe-card case full of blank three-inch by five-inch index cards, which we called Ready Eddies. Whenever Eddie was with employees and someone had a good idea or a valuable comment, he made a note of it and gave it to someone back at headquarters. In order to ensure that appropriate action would be taken, Eddie set deadlines.

If Eddie gave you one of these index cards, you had forty-eight to seventy-two hours to respond to Eddie or the individual who had made the suggestion. If you could not offer a response within that time frame, you had to send a note stating that you were working on the item and would have an answer or response by a definite date. This was one of the best systems for feedback I have ever encountered: it emanated from the CEO, it was sincere, and it was timely. It made people feel that what they said was important.

I believe that the most fundamental need possessed by human beings is the need to love and be loved. It may surprise you to learn that this is something a company can help provide. Although romantic love can sometimes be found in the workplace, this clearly falls outside the domain of company policy. On the other hand, a sense of caring and respect for the people with whom you come in contact should be as much a part of the work experience as it is in any other area of life. A work environment characterized by kindness and consideration is one in which employees feel validated. And when people feel validated, they are far more likely to do a better job.

The Encompassing Provision

Ownership and profit-sharing programs have the unique ability to satisfy, at least partially, some needs on all levels of the hierarchy. That is why I call it an encompassing provision. A salary can provide only purchasing power, but ownership and profit sharing address a person's sense of belonging, accomplishment, and need for validation.

On the basic need level, the Southwest ownership and profit-sharing plan increased purchasing power with small quarterly cash payments and ownership shares that could be turned liquid in the future. On the environment level, the profit-sharing plan created a feeling of belonging—a sense that we're all in this together.

During my tenure at Southwest, I saw pilots open their cockpit windows and yell down to someone on the ramp: "Hey, you dropped a bag there. If we run over it, we'll have to pay to have it repaired or replaced—and that comes out of profit sharing." I saw many instances where employees from different departments helped each other in extraordinary ways to get a plane out and avoid delay.

In terms of the needs hierarchy, these actions are indicative of more than a sense of belonging and teamwork. Employees felt a sense of responsibility and accountability to themselves, to each other, and to the profit-sharing program, thus satisfying some important level 4 needs. A sense of ownership creates a wonderful attitude in people. In pulling together to get every plane out on time, employees all worked toward achieving the same superordinate goal. Ownership and profit sharing can indeed create a sense of purpose and significance, thus satisfying some level 5 needs.

Because they are able to address needs at all five levels of the hierarchy, ownership and profit-sharing programs are powerful tools for creating happy and productive employees. In my view, this is one of the easiest and most effective ways for companies to take a holistic approach to satisfying employee needs.

*   *   *

Many businesses cling to a philosophy that says that a company's only obligation to employees is to provide them with a paycheck, in exchange for which an employee is obliged to return his or her best efforts on the job. As time goes on, however, more and more companies are recognizing that a salary is just the first step toward creating a productive workforce.

There are two fundamental reasons why companies must address the entire hierarchy of employee needs. In the first place, it is the ethical responsibility of a company to satisfy the needs of those whose efforts underlie its success. Human beings carry their hopes and dreams to work with them each day. A viable company is not just a mechanism for producing a product or making a dollar: it is a community and a living organism whose most valuable assets are its human resources.

The second reason that the entire hierarchy of employee needs must be addressed is pragmatic and not in the least highminded. When the needs of the people who work for a company are satisfied, they work harder and smarter. When a company's employees feel fulfilled, they become more productive—and this invariably makes for a better bottom line.

4

The Putnam Principle of Organizational Gravity

Like most kids, I used to play with building blocks. If I built a solid, simple structure, it stood indefinitely without crumbling. But when I built an edifice thirteen stories high, the slightest vibration made it wobble, and soon the whole mess tumbled to the ground. That lesson always stayed with me: the higher things are stacked, the likelier they are to fall. In fact, my youthful experience with building blocks became the basis of the Putnam principle of organizational gravity. Let's see how it pertains to structuring a business.

As the number of organizational layers in a company increases, so does the tendency to add more staff support. These include executive assistants, secretaries, and what I call "cover your rear" staff to act as buffers or padding between the layers. Before long, this kind of burgeoning bureaucracy grows out of control.

First, you need physical space to house all your surplus people. You also need office equipment, desks, benefit programs—and on and on. But even worse than these needless costs is the inefficiency that always accompanies too much bureaucracy.

When an organization becomes bloated, people lose sight of their goals, and executives and employees of bureaucratic corporations often fill up their time with work that is essentially meaningless.

A friend of mine named Bill McElman is a Chicago-based airline manager. As a young man, he spent a number of years in the U.S. Air Force—which is by any measure a formidable bureaucracy. One day, Bill didn't have much to do. So he decided that, as a joke, he would count the trays of nuts, bolts, and washers in the hangar warehouse and issue a report to his superiors.

Bill actually spent an entire day counting these tiny objects. Then he wrote a two-page report that contained a formal, itemized statement of how many nuts, bolts, and washers of various sizes were in stock. Although he received no response from his superiors, Bill repeated the same process every week for a month. Finally, he was given something more meaningful to do, so he stopped pursuing his little joke. Besides, he decided that counting nuts and bolts really wasn't that much fun—particularly since nobody else was laughing.

Another two weeks went by. Then one day Bill saw this note on his desk. It was a memo from the brass asking, "Whatever happened to the nuts, bolts, and washers report? Has someone been sleeping on the job?" Although Bill had submitted the reports as a joke and nobody had ever requested them, his superiors assumed that these reports now were necessary to their operation.

When employees identify more closely with how an organization operates than with the goals it is trying to achieve, it is a sure sign that bureaucracy has taken over. When the means of running a company obscure the ends, product quality, productivity, and employee initiative suffer and eventually fade away.

Too many bureaucratic levels create work that is every bit as unnecessary as Bill McElman's nuts, bolts, and washers reports. When that happens, corporate cancer begins to set in. It can slowly permeate any organization—and it has done so in a number of our largest and most visible corporations.

Every one of these companies has dedicated employees who are in daily contact with real customers. But instead of being supported by management, these folks are weighted down by a gigantic, unproductive organism that feeds on itself.

This kind of bureaucratic disease can be curtailed. The best solution is, of course, never to let it start: in business as in medicine, preventive measures are always easier to implement than reparative ones. But even if your company is being eaten alive by bureaucracy, there are things you can do to rescue it. The following dos and don'ts of structuring a business will give you some insight into how to avoid or repair such problems in your own companies. I'll start by contrasting the organizational styles of two corporations with which I was intimately involved—United and Southwest.

The United Way: Fat and Sassy

When I was at United, we had nine layers of management, from the top down to the front line. At the very top was the chairman of the board of directors. The chief executive officer (CEO) occupied the second level, and in the number three spot there was the chief operating officer (COO). Under him were three vice presidents who were division general managers, located in New York, Chicago, and San Francisco. Reporting to each one of those division general managers were as many as five regional vice presidents.

There was a customer service manager assigned to each airport, but that person could not physically be at the airport twenty-four hours a day. Which brings us to the seventh level—the shift manager. You can certainly understand that the shift managers needed support to handle the various aspects of the operation—such as ticketing down on the concourse and out on the ramp. So below the managers who were in charge of each shift, there was an eighth level of supervisors.

Because union contracts mandated that there be a senior or lead agent for each group of employees, a ninth level was created. We finally got to the ticket agents—the front-line employees who actually came into contact with customers.

United apparently has flattened its organizational structure in recent years, but during the time I was with that airline, we had 50,000 employees with more than eighty vice presidents. A company of that size needs a large number of senior executives to manage thousands of employees, administer satellite offices, and handle all sorts of complexities created by sheer size. Still, as I'll illustrate, such bureaucracy—if not held in check—can balloon to ridiculous proportions.

Every Monday at United, the seven most senior officers met as the corporate policy committee to amend current policy and determine new policy on all aspects of the airline. Then the information created at the corporate policy committee meeting was disseminated through the operations management committee, which met twice monthly. The OM committee flew in the divisional general managers and other personnel from the field to participate in the discussions. At that point, each divisional general manager flew home and promptly called for a division policy committee meeting to disseminate all the information they received from the OM committee. The attendance of all regional VPs was required at the division policy committee meeting.

Consider what we're talking about from the perspective of time: The corporate policy committee met every Monday, *all day*. The operations management committee met twice a month, *all day*. I also chaired a group called the system marketing council, which met with all senior marketing people in the field once a month—*all day*. Corporate policy meetings took four days a month, operations management meetings took two days a month, and system marketing meetings took one day a month: that's seven days per month consumed by meetings—and some of those meetings were held merely to coordinate various aspects of other meetings.

When the division general manager went back to his area and had his policy meeting, he requested someone from headquarters to attend. That kind of interplay and involvement can be beneficial but unfortunately meant that one or two more days per month were spent in field meetings.

There are twenty working days in an average month, and most of the executives at United spent eight to ten of those days in meetings to determine policy. That left about 50 percent of the normal working month for minor details—like implementing strategic policies and creative thinking. This imbalance between bureaucratic formality and meaningful action is, in my view, dangerous. Consider the following case.

Shortly before I left United, it was decided that a more fuel-efficient kind of plane was needed to keep the airline competitive. United had an engineering department with several hundred employees, one of whose primary responsibilities was to evaluate aircraft. Before the company purchased new airplanes, between forty and seventy people were assigned to evaluate the plane. The airline also brought in outside consultants to help them conduct an extensive financial analysis.

All sorts of minds studied the project for one to two years—at extraordinary expense. Ultimately, the committee would conclude that a particular type of aircraft was most appropriate. If you count the time it took to deliver the planes—as well as changes brought about by the duration of the study—United did not see its new equipment for three to five years from the initial decision to make such a purchase.

Think about all the shifts that can occur in the marketplace during that interval. By the time those planes arrived, another, far more fuel-efficient aircraft might become available at a better price. Unfortunately, the airline had just spent several years and untold millions of dollars acquiring aircraft that, upon delivery, could be technologically behind the times.

The lesson to be learned from this is that an industry that is highly capital intensive and requires long lead times to develop operating equipment needs nimble organization. Unless you can shorten the planning and development cycle time, you are courting trouble.

If your organization is weighed down by bureaucracy, your employees will become frustrated and lethargic, and soon this attitude will be reflected in the marketplace. If corrective measures are not taken in short order, employees become even more lethargic in their attitude and behavior, and your company will lose even more of its competitive edge.

The Southwest Way: Flat and Flexible

Lamar Muse was the first president of Southwest Airlines, and I feel he was the finest airline entrepreneur of the last forty years. From the company's inception, Muse built a flat organization with little distance between the CEO and front-line employees. Furthermore, he controlled the authority and decision-making channels within the company: To put it bluntly, the man was a dictator.

Lamar Muse led Southwest until his autocratic management

style began to impede the company's growth. There is only so far one can fly solo before the combined efforts of a team are required to generate the energy necessary to propel a company to greater heights. Unfortunately, Lamar didn't see it that way. Eventually, he forced his board of directors into a confrontation—and lost.

After I had also left Southwest, Lamar told me the story over a game of golf: "I was always arguing with another member of the board, Rollin King, one of the company's cofounders. We just couldn't agree on much in those days. Anyway, during one of the board meetings I called for a vote and said, 'Either Rollin leaves the board or I quit as president.'"

At that point Lamar left the room while the board voted. Ten minutes later, they called him back to give him the results. "Sorry, Lamar," one of the board members began, not trying very hard to appear disappointed. "You lose."

"I was shocked," Lamar admitted to me, "but at least I kept my sense of humor. When they broke the news, I just took my keys out of my pocket and threw them down on the table. Then I stared straight at them and said, 'Damn, I'd have never called for a vote if I thought I wasn't going to win,' and walked out of the room."

Shortly after Lamar Muse left Southwest, I was recruited as president and CEO. When I arrived in Dallas, I immediately formed a senior management *team.* It included all the officers who already were at Southwest, as well as me and our board chair, who was based in San Antonio. All the members of the new team had worked together for some time in a coordinated fashion and may have thought of themselves as a team. Nevertheless, there is an important distinction between vague perceptions and clearly defined realities.

By creating a formal team—and including me and the absentee chair—an already flat organization was flattened even further because all policy decisions were now made as a team. There was no more up and down from chair to CEO to president to vice president back to president to CEO to chair, and so on. Instead, we functioned as a coordinated unit.

The newly formed senior management team met every Monday morning at 9:00 A.M. Because most of the senior executives at Southwest arrived at the office around 7:30 A.M., calling a meeting for 9:00 A.M. gave each of us an opportunity to review the weekend's operations with respect to our various responsibilities. When the time came to put our heads together, everyone was prepared.

Our meetings ran for approximately two and a half hours and comprised the week's formal meetings. Minutes were taken by my secretary and distributed to everyone on the team. Action items and assignments with deadlines were always spelled out before we adjourned.

When we left our meetings at Southwest, each team member came away knowing the tasks he or she had to accomplish—which events to observe and which issues to ponder. Because so little time was wasted on superfluous talk, we were able to move quickly, nimbly, and efficiently through our agendas.

When I was CEO, Southwest was a single-aircraft airline. That aircraft was the Boeing 737-200. We did not have a permanent aircraft evaluation team. In fact, our entire engineering department consisted of a single engineer. Nevertheless, when it came time to evaluate new planes, we felt we knew our business, and we counted on (and received) tremendous support from Boeing.

A company must give special attention to the evaluation and purchase of major new operating equipment. An airline that is considering the acquisition of new aircraft needs a team fully dedicated to reviewing the qualities of the airplane under proposal before it can make an appropriate decision. This team must accurately forecast the short- and long-range needs of the company and market trends, as well as the anticipated plans of the competition—and it must move expeditiously.

At Southwest, our initial "guestimation" indicated that we might have to spend as much as $1 billion for aircraft to meet our growing needs. That kind of expenditure eventually would need board approval.

I put Phil Guthrie, our vice president of finance, in charge of the aircraft evaluation team. Other than Phil, the team included Chris terKuile, our vice president in charge of flight operation, and Jack Vidal, our vice president of maintenance. Jack had one engineer in his department, whom we also made part of the team.

In approximately four months, our team brought to me their studies and their proposal. Compare that to the two years it took

United to make a similar evaluation. The report was professional, comprehensive, logical, and straightforward. It proved that Southwest needed a new generation of aircraft in order to maintain customer service quality and to remain competitive. Furthermore, we needed to order the new aircraft immediately. Unfortunately, Boeing was not building the plane we needed—at least not yet.

Evaluation in hand, we went to Boeing. At the time Southwest was flying 737-200s, and we wanted to stay with 737s. By sticking with the same basic design we could avoid having to create an expensive separate parts inventory and fully retrain our flight and maintenance crews. We asked if Boeing would consider upgrading the current 737 and learned that they had been thinking about doing so for quite some time but no airline had shown any interest. We convinced them that our interest was sincere and immediate.

Within three months Boeing presented us full specs on a stretched 737. It was called the 737-300 and was just what Southwest needed. We presented our engine needs to General Electric and Pratt & Whitney. From the start, General Electric was very interested, but, to our surprise, Pratt & Whitney expressed no interest whatsoever.

At a black-tie affair in Seattle, held by Boeing, I introduced myself to the then-CEO of United Technologies, parent company of Pratt & Whitney, and said, "Southwest is a very successful and quickly growing regional airline. We are looking for a new airplane, and we've almost settled on Boeing's 737-300. Our initial order will be forty aircraft. We're going to need an engine—at least eighty of them. General Electric is very interested, but we can't seem to get your people at Pratt & Whitney too excited."

The CEO of United Technologies then said, arrogantly, "The future is not in small airplanes. The future is only in large airplanes—and that's where we're going to play."

As it turned out, he was wrong. The 737-300 is used by a number of airlines around the world and is powered exclusively by General Electric CFM-56-3 engines. The future was very much in small, fuel-efficient planes, and the 737-300 is but one example of that trend.

Southwest agreed to place the initial order for the 737-300, and then USAir began to consider the plane and its engines for its expansion plans. Together we secured excellent prices on the engines, with long-term price guarantees. In addition, Boeing and GE also gave us a fuel-burn guarantee: if the engine used more than a specified amount of fuel, we would be reimbursed in cash. It was a highly rewarding team effort by our people at Southwest and the folks at Boeing and General Electric.

But there was still another formidable challenge to be met before our plans could be realized. The entire proposal had to be approved by Southwest's board of directors before we could proceed. After our discussions with Boeing and GE, our recommendation to the board was to purchase ten aircraft immediately and place options on an additional thirty. That approach allowed us to avoid being stuck with forty airplanes if something drastically changed in the economy. We would lose only a small deposit.

Gene Bishop, the chairman of a large bank in Dallas, was on the Southwest board at the time. He looked at our presentation and said, "Howard, my area of expertise is finances—not airlines. I trust you, but before I commit to spending a billion dollars on this little company, I would really like to have the expert opinion of an outsider that backs up what you and your small team of warriors have shown here."

It was left up to me to select a qualified outside party to evaluate our conclusions. I needed to find a group or individual with enough experience and knowledge of the market to look at the evaluation, ask a minimum of questions, and come to a conclusion.

I did not want a group or individual that would have to perform another evaluation just to determine the validity of ours. People at GE or Boeing could do the job, but they presented a potential conflict-of-interest problem. Since both these companies had much to gain by Southwest board approval, the credibility of any conclusions reached by their employees might be called into question. I needed an unbiased opinion.

Then I remembered a man named Marvin Whitlock. Marvin had been the senior vice president in charge of engineering and maintenance at Capital, American, and United Airlines. His knowledge and experience would be perfect for evaluating our effort. Unfortunately, all I could remember about Marvin was that he had retired and moved to Santa Fe, New Mexico, some years ago. Much to my pleasant surprise, I found Marvin's phone number in the Santa Fe telephone directory. He happened to be at home when I called. "Marvin, this is Howard Putnam. What are you doing?" I asked very bluntly.

"Oh, just sitting around enjoying retirement, Howard," he answered. "What can I do for you?"

"How would you like to take on a project? I need someone to assess an aircraft evaluation my team at Southwest has done."

"I'd love to do that," he said.

The next day he flew to Dallas. When he arrived in my office, I wasted no time. I handed him the stack of books and papers related to the evaluation and said, "Marvin, what would you charge me to take these home with you, read through them, and write me a report assessing our efforts in evaluating this new aircraft purchase?"

"Well, Howard," he replied slowly, "my wife and I have grandchildren here in Dallas. If you could see your way to get us passes on Southwest once in a while to come visit them, I'd do it for $600. I'm just glad to have the opportunity to help out."

I don't know where Marvin came up with that figure, but I certainly didn't want to press my luck by asking. So I gathered some Southwest flight bags, piled all the research and reports into them, and sent Marvin back to New Mexico.

Two weeks later, I received a three-page handwritten letter from Marvin outlining his assessment of our evaluation, along with his apology for not having a typewriter. Marvin said that ours was the finest aircraft evaluation he had ever seen in all his years in the business. He asked if I would fly him to Dallas to meet the engineering group that had put it together.

When I introduced him to our four-person team, Marvin was rendered speechless. He was used to the kind of 600-strong engineering department they had at United. In any case, we again presented our evaluation to the board—this time with Marvin's handwritten letter in hand. By the meeting's end, the $1 billion purchase of aircraft had been approved.

From that point, Southwest grew very quickly. In the three years we were there, the company tripled in size and profitability.

As we continued to widen our network, we refused to get caught in the trap of bureaucratic hierarchy. During my tenure at the airline, we added only three new officer positions—and those were in areas that we considered to be absolutely essential.

How to Cut the Fat

I like to compare a company's organizational strength to the body of an athlete. Whatever the sport, all athletes are prepared to perform at their best when their bodies are lean and fit. The same basic principle applies to business. For a company to operate at its optimum level, it must trim away the fat that can bog it down and eventually cause its demise.

Reducing bureaucracy affects every aspect of an operation, including customer service, employee morale, shareholder value, profitability, competitiveness, and product quality. Each company must pinpoint the areas where it needs to trim organizationally, but certain specific places should be looked at first for fat. Here are some guidelines:

MANAGEMENT

Reduce Layers and Numbers

The primary cause of bureaucracy is stacked management. I have a three-step approach to solving this problem: reduce the number of layers; then reduce the raw numbers within those remaining layers; finally, if at all possible, eliminate the concept of layers.

Trimming organizational layers is something that every company has to consider—whether it is experiencing growth, decline, or crisis. At Southwest we had a policy of no assistants. Officers and senior managers were assigned a person who handled traditional secretarial responsibilities but no administrative or executive assistants. I considered this to be a preemptive reduction of excess layers: we eliminated them before they could be added.

Braniff, however, presented a completely different situation.

Excess layers of management had been installed long before I came on board, and the first step in restructuring that company was to remove those superfluous levels—starting at the top.

When there are too many people at the head of an organization, it becomes top-heavy and unwieldy, and a lot of people are required at lower levels to function as support. Too many people at the top make it difficult for a company to move quickly and efficiently. In an emergency situation—such as the one we faced at Braniff—there is no time for long delays in decision making; in a healthy situation there is no need for it. A key tenet of the Putnam principle of organizational gravity is this: reduce the size of the head, and you reduce the weight of the entire organizational body.

When my financial officer Phil Guthrie and I looked at Braniff's big picture, we saw too much senior management. We agreed that if we took immediate steps to cut back in this area, the company would have a much better chance of righting itself.

We started by eliminating fourteen staff vice presidents, none of whom had field or line responsibility. We also did away with most of the regional vice presidents and shift-manager positions in operations. We kept the executive vice president of operations because the position was necessary and the gentleman was good at his job, but when the executive vice president of marketing resigned, we did not replace him. Since my background is in marketing, I felt I could handle those responsibilities and had his people report directly to me.

Within a few months, Braniff's ten organizational levels were condensed to a much more fit six. We accomplished this by eliminating the superfluous layers of management—along with the redundant and unnecessary procedures and policies that they generated. Because decision making was tight and not loosely spread throughout the corporation, we had greater control over what occurred within the company—and in the marketplace. As a result, the entire process became far more efficient.

In evaluating your own company, start by looking at the organizational layers that have been installed over the years. Ask yourself why they were put in place and what they are now contributing to the company. Were certain layers or departments set up to deal with a particular situation that no longer exists? Do they add value? Could they contribute more, or would it be better to cut them out completely? Making these decisions will help you keep your business lean and prepared for the unpredictable.

Install Accountability

As you evaluate the best ways to trim the fat from your organization, try to pinpoint where people or positions are under-utilized, so that you can make the best use of each team member. Beyond the actual size of an organization, you also have to think about the *way* in which things are structured. One key to a lean and fit company is accountability. In other words, who is responsible for what?

Once you can answer that question, you can eliminate the kind of buck passing and scapegoating that accompany bureaucratic irresponsibility. Making people accountable helps them understand and value their roles in building a successful company. Don't be afraid to encourage your people to display more initiative. Talented men and women welcome the opportunity to show their stuff. The more responsibility you give them, the more they—and your company—will thrive. This works at all employee levels.

COMMUNICATION

Establish Open and Direct Communication

I find that things happen faster and much more the way you intended when you talk with people face to face, one on one. My personal policy has always been that if I needed to talk to Joe Smith in accounting, I went and talked to Joe Smith—even if there were two other people between us in terms of the corporate chain of command. I learned early in my corporate life that if I sent something through all the relay stations, it was apt to be miscommunicated or misinterpreted, leading to additional work down the road to clear up the matter.

If there were changes to be made in an administrative procedure, however, I went through the appropriate vice president or department head and at times joined the discussion with the appropriate front-line manager. But for the most part it was the vice president's responsibility to implement the changes, and he or she was accountable. Everyone understood, however, that we were all free—and encouraged—to visit and collect input directly from men and women at any level.

In a bureaucratic-style chain of command, some folks get all bent out of shape by all this freedom of movement. But I never felt resentment from my department heads because they knew that I would never undermine their authority.

Whenever I was given the opportunity to lead an organization, I encouraged all my people to talk directly to the man or woman who had immediate responsibility for the issue at hand. If employees on the front line were concerned about the direction of the company or its policies, they were encouraged to come straight to me. I requested their input—and they felt free to seek mine.

Rather than issuing memos or requesting meetings, when I have something to say, I'll pick up the phone or walk to the person's office and deliver my message. I realize that an open-door style of management can become dysfunctional if it is burdened with unnecessary "friendly" interruptions or repeated disturbances by incompetent individuals. But if handled correctly, it is one of the best ways to instill a sense of teamwork.

By staying visible and involved, I was able to demonstrate to my employees my concern with their welfare—as well as the welfare of the company. One day at Braniff, when the crisis had reached its worst, I put on coveralls and showed up unannounced at Dallas–Fort Worth Airport to help load baggage and cargo. This gesture had far greater impact than a hundred memos or meetings in terms of what it did for the morale of the folks on the front line.

Open communication is also important externally—in terms of what you say to the press and to your creditors, shareholders, and the general public. As CEO, I felt it was my responsibility to be accountable for both the good and the bad news. I was the company's primary spokesperson: I met the press. I talked with the public. I went to Wall Street to keep the investment community current.

Here again, when the information comes "right from the horse's mouth," there is less opportunity for misunderstanding or confusion. In addition, I always made certain that at least three other senior officers were sufficiently well versed to make a statement if I happened to be unavailable. At no time did we use the all-too-common unnamed spokesperson.

Eliminate Jargon from All Forms of Communication

Few things are more indicative of what's wrong with bureaucracies than statements that are written or spoken in legalese, financialese, or computerese. The same goes for defensive statements cloaked in corporate propaganda and doublespeak.

Unless the information you are trying to convey demands a specific kind of technical language, eliminate all hyperbole and five-dollar words from your written and spoken messages. By taking this simple step, you will make your communications more effective—and far more believable.

Use the Power of the Promise to Affirm Your Commitments

There is something about bureaucracies that makes it difficult for people to state their needs and intentions directly. I grew up in an era when business was done by a handshake: your word was your bond. But as time goes on, we seem to have forgotten the power of the promise.

I'm not saying that people are less honest than they once were, but I find that men and women hesitate more to make a solid commitment. This is particularly true in bureaucratic corporations.

I've always been a firm believer in the power of the promise. This power can be activated by using straightforward, affirmative language in everything you write and say. A company's leader needs to set a positive example for his or her people as someone who makes and keeps promises. This kind of affirmative action has far more impact than impersonal policy statements issued from above.

One of the most important examples of the power of the promise involves doing things when you say you are going to do them—which brings us back to the question of deadlines. Everything worth doing needs to be done within a specific time frame. Deadlines force people to use their time efficiently. "I'll have this report on your desk on Wednesday" has a much different ring to it than "I'll do my best to complete the report within the next few weeks—if time permits."

I've had ample opportunity to observe these two approaches to commitment—and each one's long-term effect on morale and productivity. There's no question in my mind that the use of promises and deadlines creates a sense of urgency and immediacy, while wishy-washy statements and loose commitments make a company lazy and unresponsive.

PRODUCT LINE AND PRODUCT PRICES

Trim the Product Line

A product line must be evaluated and managed like any other element of your business. One way to determine whether your product line is appropriate is to examine each product individually to see whether it is forwarding your company's objectives. A similar evaluation also should be made for your product line as a whole.

If you determine that a particular product is not profitable, you have to ask yourself why you should continue to produce it: prestige, tradition, laziness, fear? Let me show you why these are not very good reasons to continue with it.

Laziness and fear are motivations that seldom propel companies toward anything positive. Greater prestige can generally be found in products that make money. New traditions can always be started by creative leaders.

I've seen too many companies continue to produce products out of habit and inertia. This can be a fatal mistake. It is essential that you constantly evaluate and review your product line to determine whether it still makes sense for the consumer—and for your company.

At one point during my tenure at Braniff, we cut first-class service out of our product line. We determined that it didn't support or forward our superordinate goal of being the low-cost trunk carrier. Perhaps even more important, this product line was losing money. Every dollar we earned through first class cost $1.50 to produce. Most of our first-class seats were usually filled with employees, discount upgrades, and people riding on some sort of pass.

How do you determine which products to trim? First, check to see whether the product in question helps you reach the superordinate goal of your company. If the answer is no, ask yourself why you are producing or offering it. If you can't come up with a satisfactory reply, consider trimming that product line or cutting it out completely.

If you determine that a particular product is forwarding the objectives of your company, ask yourself how well it is contributing to that goal relative to your other products. Check sales, inventory, returns, and consumer complaints. Stay apprised of all statistics and market conditions that pertain to the product—and to your product line as a whole. Once you are armed with this information, you will be in a good position to determine which products should stay and which should go.

Simplify Pricing

One of the first things that struck me on my arrival at Braniff was the airline's complex pricing system: it was burdening the company financially by needlessly tying up both personnel and customers on the phone and at ticket counters. Braniff's fare structure included 578 different fares, yet it didn't offer more than fifteen different flying experiences. Basically, an airline has peak and off-peak times, a couple of different classes, and a lot of destinations that fall into several large zones. The primary commodity it offers customers is a seat.

One Sunday we sat down and slashed Braniff's price structure from 578 to fifteen. The reduction in the attendant paperwork was dramatic. Customer service became far more efficient: we doubled the number of phone reservations and in-person ticket transactions we could process without adding additional personnel and cut our administrative costs almost in half.

I urge you to take a long and careful look at your pricing. Ask yourself the following questions:

- Does your pricing structure make the decision process quicker and easier for your customers?
- Does your pricing structure reflect what is happening in the marketplace?
- Does your pricing structure create redundancies in accounting and administration?
- Does your pricing structure tie up your people with paperwork instead of activities that generate sales?
- Does your pricing structure contribute or take away from your superordinate goal and your bottom line?

If your answer to one or more of these questions causes you to reevaluate your pricing strategies, I hope you will have the foresight and courage to do whatever it takes to make your pricing work *for* you—not against you.

Always Make the Customer Your Primary Consideration

Product lines that do not address customer satisfaction threaten the future of your company. Products of low or mediocre quality, produced out of convenience or laziness, demonstrate that an organization's leaders lack courage, creativity, and innovation. Companies that are bogged down in bureaucracy are often propelled by fear, ignorance, and a blind devotion to tradition. The key to a profitable company is customer satisfaction: it must remain foremost in a company's decision-making process. My feeling is that if a product taxes the bottom line and does not satisfy customers, eliminate it as quickly as possible.

CONCLUSION

In comparing a business to the human body, flatness equals fitness. A company that is fit and lean is more agile, more proactive, and more responsive to ever-changing circumstances.

Because they are lean and fit, flat organizations are able to negotiate more easily through all sorts of turbulence. They can change as quickly as the environment. At its best, a lean and fit organization often anticipates many of those changes even before they occur. This, by definition, is the very antithesis of a bureaucracy.

Flat companies have unique advantages in four critical areas:

1. Customer service

   Flat companies have less distance between customers and senior management.

   By empowering front-line employees, flat companies can better communicate with customers.

2. Competitiveness

   Flat companies are more innovative and better able to respond to changing conditions.

   Flat companies are better able to evaluate the competition and reposition themselves in the market.

3. Management

   Flat companies can more easily meet the needs of their employees because they have no unnecessary team members.

   Flat companies have more powerful and empowering networks throughout the organization.

4. Administration

   Flat companies have lower overhead.

   Flat companies have less redundancy of effort.

   Because there are fewer levels to coordinate, flat companies are more easily integrated.

For now, a flat organization is the best way to go. But remember, the organizational models and attitudes that work today may eventually be obsolete. By the time the flat model is fully understood, something better and more innovative will emerge to take its place. Pursue vigorously new paradigms and models for thought and action. Try to anticipate trends and changes before they occur. Stay fit and alert—and always be ready for anything. The life of your company may depend on it!

5

In 100 Words or Less: Keep Your Strategy Short, Sweet, and Simple

What business are you in?

I think most of you would agree that this is just about the most fundamental question you can ask any executive, manager, or entrepreneur—at least that's how it first appears. But let me offer a case in point that demonstrates part of the reason that this whole issue is more complicated than it may look.

Some of you may be familiar with Avon products. Avon is a well-known cosmetics company that once had a veritable army of women going door-to-door selling its products all over the country. The slogan it used in radio and TV ads started out with the ding-dong of a doorbell and a woman who said, "Hello. Avon calling."

If I were to ask you what business Avon was in, you would probably say cosmetics. But in a sense, you would be wrong. Although it is certainly true that the products Avon dispensed were cosmetics, the company was actually in the communication—or gossip—business.

The peak period of Avon's door-to-door business was before the days of giant suburban malls and TV services like the Home Shopping Network. People in many parts of the country lived miles away from the nearest major shopping center and did much of their shopping through catalogs or during infrequent and time-consuming trips to a neighboring city or town. So the woman from Avon was providing a valuable service—bringing cosmetics right to the door, along with free product samples and gifts. But now you're probably wondering where the communication part comes in.

That Avon representative became an important part of a home-maker's gossip network because, along with the perfume and lipstick, came news about all the neighbors. "I was just over at the Wilson's house down the street," the saleswoman would say, as a customer was deciding which cosmetics to order. "They just bought a beautiful new living room set. By the way, I think their oldest daughter is about to become engaged." Three weeks later, when the saleswoman returned to deliver the order, she was sure to have an update about the neighbors: "It looks like the Wilson girl is going to tie the knot this coming summer."

Naturally, all of Avon's customers believed that they were dealing with a cosmetics company and that the local gossip delivered by the saleswoman was just an attractive fringe benefit. But you can be sure that the policymakers and managers at Avon—as well as each and every salesperson—understood the nature of their company's unique value to customers. This simple sense of purpose sets the stage for the kind of strategy every business needs to succeed.

What about you? Are you aware of your company's underlying mission—and its unique value to the customers it serves? Many businesspeople do not have a clear vision of the nature and purpose of their companies—a fact that was first brought home to me at Harvard University.

The Mission Statement

The year was 1978, and I was group vice president of marketing for United Airlines. I was selected to spend thirteen weeks attending the Advanced Management Program at Harvard Business School, studying some 200 corporate case histories and trying with other senior executives to devise innovative solutions to a variety of business problems. Living and collaborating with a group of successful and talented executives from every imaginable field—sharing stories and experiences, comparing notes—I learned a great deal about how companies operate and how their strengths and weaknesses contribute to their successes and failures. The critical difference between companies that thrived and those that struggled hinged on the clarity and vision of their basic strategies.

Many companies were confused about their strategic position and marketing direction, and to pinpoint the cause of that confusion, I decided to conduct a survey of the people who were attending the Harvard program with me. I asked the following question: "Can you—in 100 words or less—describe the essence of your corporation's strategy and unique vision?"

A large percentage of the senior executives to whom I posed this question could not offer a clear statement of their company's mission. Some hesitated or countered my question with one of their own. Others meandered through half-hearted, unfocused statements on quality control or long-term profit planning. Only a few were able quickly to respond with the kind of concise, well-conceived statement that underlies the success of any business.

Try to answer the same basic question I asked my colleagues at Harvard: "Can you—in 100 words or less—describe the essence of your corporation's strategy and unique vision?"

Don't feel bad if you find it difficult to respond with a definitive answer: you've got plenty of company. As I speak to groups of executives and businesspeople around the country, many bright and highly motivated men and women are unable to define the nature and mission of their businesses. One of my missions in writing this book is to help you formulate a clear strategy with which to build a successful company.

When I have led corporations, my leadership has been based on a simple strategy that everybody in the organization understands and embraces. A concise statement of purpose comes right from the top, supported by the senior management team's mission statement and a lengthy and detailed strategic plan.

Shortly after I took over as president of Southwest Airlines, we formulated the following mission statement and sent a copy to every executive, manager, and front-line employee:

The mission of Southwest Airlines is to provide safe and comfortable air transportation in commuter and short-haul markets, from close-in airports, at prices competitive with automobiles and busses, and to involve customers and employees in the product and the process, making the airline a fun, profitable, and quality experience for all.

The mission statement at Southwest was fifty-two words long and covered our niche, market, competition, pricing, and financial goals. It also addressed the needs of our customers and employees, as well as our basic values and the kind of working atmosphere we wanted to achieve.

I strongly suggest that you make it a priority to produce a similar statement about your company. Think of your mission statement as a declaration of your company's intent—its reason for being in business. And don't worry too much about adjustments or changes that you may have to make in the future. Just deal with what is in your control right now—while keeping apprised of conditions that may compel you to alter your basic strategy. Most successful business leaders are committed to their present strategy and flexible enough to alter it in response to changing conditions.

I'm reminded of a story about a young fisherman who spotted an older fisherman across the lake. The young man noticed that every time the older guy landed a fish, he measured his catch. If the fish he snared was over eight inches long, the old man threw it back into the lake.

The young fisherman greeted the older man: "Most of the people who fish on this lake keep the big ones and throw back the little ones. That way, we get a nice big fish for dinner, and the small ones get a chance to grow up and become big fish that we can catch and eat later on."

"Sound reasoning, young fella," the old fisherman said.

"But for some reason you keep the small fish and throw back the big ones," the young man continued. "Can you tell me why?"

"Because I've got a frying pan that's only eight inches across, and the bigger fish don't fit," the old fisherman said matter-of-factly.

"Why don't you just get a bigger frying pan?" the younger man asked.

"Because I've always used this one. Been using this same frying pan for twenty-five years. Why should I change now?"

I've seen this same kind of rigid approach stifle or destroy many companies. Like the old fisherman, businesspeople sometimes resist correcting their strategy in response to evolving conditions for a very simple reason: they dislike change.

In today's fast-moving business climate, you had better be prepared to deal with the unknown—or you may inadvertently be tossing that big fish back into the water.

Flexibility in an organization—or an individual—is a prerequisite to success. Simplicity of purpose allows for that flexibility. A company with a simple plan and a simple organizational structure can adapt quickly to both positive and negative conditions. That kind of agility and readiness is reflected in the 100-word-or-less mission statement.

The basics of creating a clear and forceful mission statement include the following:

1. Write your statement in 100 words or less. Make sure it clearly declares your company's purpose and basic strategy.

2. Whatever the size of your company, the mission statement must emanate from the CEO or senior officer. It must then be shared with—and affirmed by—every employee. The statement must create an esprit de corps—a winning attitude that permeates every aspect of the operation.

3. At some point in the statement, you should define an overriding goal that is attractive to employees, customers, and shareholders. A few words about the company's ethics and values also should be included in this section.

4. Build some kind of rewards system into your strategy. Employees have to feel that if they work harder and smarter, there will be something in it for them on the other side.

5. Ensure that you are still in the right market niche—and not passing up opportunities to improve your service or product—by implementing a strategy that allows for feedback from employees and customers.

The Strategic Plan

The mission statement reflects a company's decision about the direction in which it wants to travel en route to its ultimate destination. In a way, it's like planning a trip to a particular place. Although it is essential to know where you're going before starting out on a journey, you are not likely to get very far unless you have a map to guide you there. That is the main purpose of the strategic plan.

The strategic plan is the map a company charts based on the goals it sets in its mission statement. Through it, an executive filters all proposed actions to see whether they will advance the goals of the company. If so, the executive proceeds. If not, the executive stops and thinks, "This proposal doesn't fit in with our mission and therefore is not acceptable at this time" or "Although it's not included in our stated goals, maybe we ought to think about reevaluating our basic strategy."

Like every element of business in these turbulent times, the strategic plan must be flexible. It also needs to be direct, comprehensive, cohesive, succinct—and, above all, empowering to those who are responsible for its implementation.

At Southwest, our strategic plan had ten essential points. The entire statement fit on two double-spaced, typewritten pages. Like our mission statement, it was spelled out in plain English and was easy to understand. I'd like to share those ten points with you—with some comments and observations that I hope will be helpful.

NICHE AND MARKETS

Southwest will fly segments of 600 miles or less in the southwest quadrant of the United States with enough frequency of service to fulfill commuter needs. In markets of 350 miles or less, Southwest will fly seven round trips daily, and in markets of 350 miles or more, four round trips daily. To avoid delays and excess ground time, Southwest will accept only small-package freight.

At Southwest, we made a distinction between ourselves and other airlines: we were *not* in the airline business; we were in the mass transportation business. Our prices were so low that we became a viable alternative to traveling by car, bus, or train.

Southwest had positioned itself as an alternative to a family's front porch. "It's so inexpensive to fly Southwest," one of our ads said, "that you really can't afford to stay home." By inventing this new niche in the market, we developed a customer base that none of our competitors had tapped. But creating a successful niche is not the same as maintaining it.

Once a company has carved out a viable market position, it can easily fall into the trap of becoming complacent and self-satisfied. This can be a fatal mistake. All niches are temporary. They either erode, disappear, or evolve into other niches.

Several years ago, I watched a company successfully capitalize on a niche and watched as that same company spiraled toward financial disaster. The company, OshKosh B'Gosh, made a killing in the manufacture and sales of children's overalls that were designed in the style of those worn by railroad engineers, dairy farmers, and painters. It discovered a distinct and profitable position in the market but forgot that even the best business strategies cannot last forever.

Originally, OshKosh had made workwear for adults, and the children's versions began as novelties. Then the 1980s saw an unexpected vogue in children's trousers—and suddenly OshKosh had a winner.

OshKosh found almost immediate success within its new niche and quickly changed its strategy. Previously, 85 percent of the company's sales had been in adult work clothes; now 85 percent of its sales were in children's clothes. So great was the demand for thematic children's clothing that sales rose tenfold in less than ten years. OshKosh built fifteen new plants and made a lot of children's overalls and a lot of money—for a time.

In the euphoria of its success, OshKosh failed to evaluate the marketplace objectively. During the ten years that OshKosh saw its profits leap, the base of children for whom those overalls had been purchased had quietly shrunk.

OshKosh sustained growth by filling its niche to saturation. But once the market topped out, growth stopped. As the market continued to shrink, so did the company's revenues. Before long, OshKosh was losing money and closing plants. Because this company was not prepared to deal with changes in the market, it suddenly found itself in the midst of a crisis. It had moved from the Alpha state into Beta quickly and without any contingency plans.

To avoid the kind of trouble OshKosh experienced, you must constantly study the marketplace and review the premises on which your strategic plan is based. OshKosh did this when they switched their strategy from work clothes to children's clothes. But they got lazy the second time around. Success came so rapidly and in such a big way they thought themselves bulletproof. Fortunately, OshKosh was able to flex, scramble, restructure, and remain a viable entity, once again moving into a state of new Alpha.

When strategies are exhausted or niches disappear, companies can find themselves in a position similar to that of OshKosh. To avoid this, a company must create a living strategy—one that can be reshaped to meet all sorts of changes in the market. And conditions may warrant that it is in a company's best interests to phase out a current strategy—as it develops new ones.

FINANCIAL VIABILITY

Southwest will be the low-cost operator in the industry. It will achieve a return on equity of 30 percent, a pretax profit margin of 20 percent, and a debt-to-equity ratio of one to one.

A company must be committed to establishing and maintaining the kind of financial viability that can carry it through all sorts of ups and downs—both in its specific market as well as in the broader economy.

Most businesses experience a cash crisis at some point—often during their infancy. When the folks who are forming a company do not fully think through their financial objectives, they can easily underestimate the capital necessary for start-up. Soon they go beyond their projected financial plan, and liquidity becomes a major problem.

Young companies often incur cash crises by expanding too rapidly—and taking on too much debt in the process. The 1980s taught us that debt can impede growth, productivity, and profitability—and often result in failure and bankruptcy.

Early in Southwest's history, the company experienced a cash crunch. To stay in business, the airline sold one of its four planes. The corporation's senior officer at the time was its first president, Lamar Muse—a man who recognized the importance of sticking to a long-range plan.

Even though Southwest was experiencing serious cash problems, Lamar remained committed to the airline's goals in the areas of financial viability, flight frequency, customer service, productivity, and quality. Southwest not only stayed in business during its cash crisis, but it managed to meet most of its goals during that period. In fact, the company actually exceeded it productivity goals—setting a new standard for preparing a plane for take-off.

It was a challenge for a small airline that started out with only four planes to maintain a high level of productivity in the face of a 25 percent reduction in its operating equipment. To maintain the same number of flights with three planes as it had with four, ground times were reduced to ten minutes for complete deplaning, servicing, and reboarding for 112 passengers. This new standard in productivity became known throughout the airline industry as the ten-minute turnaround. It was an innovation that was created because of a cash crisis.

Companies typically project that they will remain financially viable if they can withstand a 10 to 15 percent drop in revenue. In light of the volatile financial times in which we live, such declines should not be considered extraordinary. We have learned through hard experience that a company should be prepared to withstand revenue drops of 25 and even 50 percent if it wants to ensure its continued viability. This is especially true for companies that are trying to survive in a declining industry—or in the face of a widespread economic downturn, such as the one we in Texas suffered during the 1980s.

A company needs to have a manageable debt that can be adequately serviced out of cash flow—as well as the ability to quickly downsize in the face of adversity—if it is going to profitably weather the turbulence it is certain to experience during the coming years.

ORGANIZATIONAL STRUCTURE

Southwest will be a flat and lean organization working as a networked team. Levels will include CEO, department heads, managers, and supervisors. A fifth level may be approved in certain departments. The Senior Management Committee, composed of all officers, will be the governing body of the day-to-day operation. The board of directors will review all major policy areas.

A company must set forth, in its strategic plan, the type of organization it wants and how it wants the organization managed. Also needed is a general—but direct—statement of your intended management style, such as the reference in the above statement to "a flat and lean organization working as a networked team."

We've seen how companies burdened with too many organizational layers can become bogged down in unessential work and unnecessary expenditures. A cumbersome company can also be compared to an unhealthy body that eventually becomes vulnerable to any number of diseases—some of them fatal.

When I worked at United Airlines, it had nine levels of management before the front line. In terms of communication, financial planning, and true activity, a company that has too many layers between its top executives and the employees who are in daily touch with its customers is going to have a hard time responding quickly and effectively.

I have found that the best-run organizations are flat. They function with a few meaningful and well-coordinated levels, accelerating decision making and avoiding waste and bureaucracy. Perhaps most important, this kind of organizational approach stays responsive to the needs of its customers, while keeping its employees challenged and motivated to work for the betterment of the team.

A good example of a flat organization in action is a group of firefighters standing around a safety net, trying to catch a person who is falling off a building. Each one of those firefighters may have a different rank—chief, captain, sergeant—but they're all pitching in and pulling their own weight as parts of a coordinated unit.

ETHICS AND VALUES

At Southwest, we will operate by the Golden Rule. This applies to our relationships with all constituencies—including employees, customers, suppliers, lenders, and shareholders. As a company and as individuals, we will not tolerate dishonesty, stealing, maliciousness, or deceit.

A company's sense of ethics needs to be reflected in all its procedures and policies—as well as in the thoughts and actions of employees. Ethics must begin with the CEO and emanate outward to each employee and every circumstance in which employees may find themselves. Ethical behavior must remain a constant through good or bad economic times.

A company's values must be part of a living, breathing system. They cannot exist only as platitudes presented in speeches or glossy pamphlets. A company's ethics (or lack of ethics) is reflected in everything the leaders of that company say and do.

When a corporation produces poor-quality products or does not honor its commitments, employees take this behavior as a model for their own performance. When the CEO and other leaders are not truthful with the media or the general public, employees assume that such behavior is also acceptable on their part.

In the 1980s a number of ruthless businesspeople became popular media figures, but I believe that this fascination with people and companies that achieve success at any price has peaked. Today, the public wants to deal with corporations that stand behind their services and products—as well as their people. I believe that as we approach the new century, those business leaders who minimize the importance of ethics and values will find their indifference reflected in the bottom line.

COMMITMENT TO STAKEHOLDERS

At Southwest, we realize our investors, employees, and customers depend on us. All stakeholders will benefit, in some way, from our profitability. In particular, after one year of service, employees will become part of a profit-sharing and stock-ownership plan.

A stakeholder is anyone who stands to benefit by a company's prosperity. Stakeholders depend on a company to succeed, just as the company depends on its stakeholders.

The more kinds of stakeholders a company can bring under its umbrella, the greater its potential for long-term prosperity. When a company demonstrates concern and support for its stakeholders, those actions are returned in kind.

Employee support ensures that a company's products and services are of high quality. Customer support keeps the dollars rolling in. Investor support pays for research and expansion. Supplier support can be indispensable in times of cash crunches. Community support integrates the company into a larger context.

The support of stakeholders can keep a company thriving, but such support must be nurtured through actions that convey mutual respect and commitment. A company demonstrates its commitment to employees through job stability and a profit-sharing and ownership plan. Commitment to community is demonstrated through contributions of time, money, or facilities. Commitment to suppliers is reflected by a company's continued use of those products and services.

One autumn, a new competitor, Texas International, arrived at Dallas's Love Field. The competitor challenged Southwest's route to Houston's Intercontinental Airport. Our fares were already low and our service excellent. Although Southwest was in fine shape at the time, we felt that we had to do something in response to this new challenge.

We came up with a surprisingly simple answer involving a stakeholder that many companies mistakenly neglect—the community.

For sixty days before Christmas, Southwest contributed one dollar to the Dallas Salvation Army and the Dallas Handicapped

Recreation Department for every passenger boarded from Dallas Love Field to Houston Intercontinental Airport. Customers already liked our service, but now they saw a special reason to fly Southwest. Company and customer pulled together and the community benefited by over $50,000. By the way, our competitor never gained a foothold and soon left Dallas.

CUSTOMER SERVICE

Customer complaints will not exceed one per 100,000 passengers boarded. Eighty-five percent of all our flights will arrive within fifteen minutes of schedule. Ninety percent of Southwest's planes will have ground times no longer than ten minutes. Cash-register-type passenger tickets and simplified check-in and baggage handling are a must. Southwest will not interline baggage or tickets.

Much of the quality of our customer service was a direct result of our productivity goals. Our ten-minute turnaround ensured passengers of a speedy departure. Our cash-register tickets reduced the time and trouble of boarding. Our flight crews received payment per trip, not per hour. This incentive ensured passengers the speediest trip possible.

From 60 to 70 percent of all customers lost by a service-oriented business leave because of rude or indifferent service. In the case of an airline, one such unpleasant incident is often enough to make a passenger look elsewhere when it comes time to take that next flight.

It costs twice as much to secure a customer as it does to keep one. That's why it's essential that employees—especially those who come into immediate contact with the public—understand their vital role in implementing this key aspect of your strategy. Courtesy and respect for the customer are essential. Beyond that, your criteria for the quality of customer service you aim to provide should be explicit and memorized by every employee.

TOOLS OF THE TRADE

Southwest will fly only the Boeing 737-200 and 737-300 aircraft. This will maintain efficiency of scheduling, offer consistency, require only one inventory of spare parts, and limit additional training of maintenance and flight crews for different aircraft.

Shortly after my arrival at Southwest, several years of ongoing litigation with Braniff concluded in Southwest's favor. As part of the settlement, Southwest received the chance to lease aircraft from Braniff at reduced rates. The lease price was so low that we decided to take advantage of the opportunity. As an experiment, we tested the larger capacity 727-200 for our short-haul business, even though our strategy did not include using this type of aircraft.

The basic tenet of a living strategic plan is flexibility. That's why we elected to experiment with the 727. Some CEOs would wonder why a company that was doing so well would risk trying something new, but such a philosophy leaves little room for innovation and progress.

One key to effective management—particularly in these turbulent times—is an openness to change, even when no changes seem to be necessary. The 727 experiment is an example of proactive thought and leadership. Southwest did not need a new kind of aircraft—yet we looked at one when the opportunity presented itself. If the 727 had proved useful, we would have incorporated it into our strategic plan. Since this was not the case, we continued to follow our original strategy.

PRODUCTIVITY GOALS

Southwest flight crews are paid by the trip—not by the hour—to encourage productivity and on-time operation. We will have a ten-minute turnaround for our aircraft. Southwest Airlines will purchase new aircraft only if it can maximize their use.

In addition to its productivity goals, a company should briefly—but specifically—define maximum use of its assets in this part of the strategic plan. Such assets include people, plant, equipment, and capital.

Southwest's most challenging productivity goal developed while the airline was experiencing a severe cash shortage. Although prior to my arrival the company was forced to sell a plane in order to stay in business, the airline made a commitment to continue offering the same service. During this crisis the company instituted the ten-minute turnaround.

The success of the ten-minute turnaround was due to its superordinate quality. This one overriding goal drove every action and every objective that related to preparing a plane for flight—including refueling, maintenance, cleaning, loading bags, and boarding passengers.

The intent of the ten-minute turnaround was to allow Southwest to transport the same number of passengers with three airplanes instead of four. What the company did not immediately realize was that the ten-minute turnaround would also serve as a powerful motivator that inspired people to reach unexpected levels of productivity.

Several years after the initiation of the ten-minute turnaround, we calculated how much money the procedure had saved the airline. We determined that it would take three additional 737s to transport the same number of people with the standard twenty-minute turnaround that was used by most airlines. Therefore, we saved the cost of three 737s and the debt service that went with them. Southwest saved $6 million annually in interest alone—not to speak of the $60 million that the three jets would have cost. This is the kind of financial impact a single superordinate productivity goal can have.

Southwest also put into place a strong productivity goal for its flight crews. Their goal was to get planes in safely and on time. Their incentive was payment per trip—not per hour. The more trips pilots or flight attendants flew, the more money they earned.

Productivity does not, as many people seem to think, result simply from working harder. Often it results from working smarter. At Southwest, productivity translated into working more efficiently with simpler procedures. For example, we used cash-register-style tickets that did not specify the passenger's name. This meant that the employee at the ticket counter could eliminate one step in each transaction.

To avoid writing the passenger's name at check-in, the gate agent simply asked passengers to say their name into a tape recorder. This created what we called a "voice manifest" of passengers and further shortened transaction time.

You might find it amusing to learn that at Southwest we experimented with increasing the productivity of our passengers. We wanted to see whether the kind of music we played in the jetways influenced the pace at which people boarded. We tried waltzes, operas, and rock music. Our findings showed that "The Lone Ranger theme from the "William Tell Overture" was the music that made passengers move most briskly. The majority of our passengers didn't even notice the music, but subliminally the marching rhythm quickened their pace. Although we eventually did away with using music during boarding, this experiment points out that a variety of things can be done to enhance productivity—if you and your people take a creative approach to the process.

PRODUCT MANAGEMENT

Southwest will offer only a single class of service. We will offer complimentary beverages on peak fares, but meals will not be served. We will have two fare levels: peak or executive, offered during the day, Monday through Friday; and off-peak or pleasure, offered on Monday through Friday evenings and weekends. Fares will be the lowest in the industry, consistent with our low-cost structure.

Product management includes two elements—product line and product pricing—and our strategic plan addressed both. Our prices would be the lowest, and we would offer two products to the customer—commuter transportation for the business traveler and transportation for the pleasure traveler. A third product, much smaller in volume but very profitable, was the small-package service. Businesses predominantly used this service, and it always came second to passengers in our planning.

As I mentioned earlier, Southwest made a distinction between itself and other airlines: we were not in the airline business; we were in the mass-transportation and commuter business. This distinction allowed us to create products that coincided with our different view. Viewing ourselves as unique created energy that was reflected in every aspect of our operation. It helped us be successful at inventing a new niche and a new customer base.

It is no longer enough simply to fight with competitors to gain a bigger share of an existing market. Successful companies need the ability to invent their own future by creating new strategies and new niches.

By inventing a new market position, Southwest gave itself three distinct advantages over its competitors. First, we were the lowest-cost operator in the industry. This advantage is difficult to beat in any business. Second, we operated only out of those airports that were close to the cities that we served. Third, our philosophy was to increase market share through new customers—rather than trying to take them away from other airlines.

Many companies operate with a more adversarial spirit, but at Southwest we believed that the pie was big enough for everyone. When we created a new market—of flights that would not exceed 300 miles—we wound up doubling the size of that market in a year. As a result, everybody benefited—we did, our customers did, and so did our competitors.

Southwest succeeded at creating products that were responsive to an ever-changing market. The airline examined its product line to determine how it could better serve its customers. An effective business leader must always keep a company's strategy flexible enough to capitalize quickly on a new niche. He or she also must have the courage and foresight to discontinue any product or service that is no longer profitable.

An example of such product flexibility occurred at a restaurant I frequent in Dallas. One day I went into the restaurant and asked for a chili dog with extra onions.

"I'm sorry, sir, we don't have chili dogs anymore," the waitress said.

"But I liked your chili dogs," I responded, disappointed.

"Well, there just weren't enough of you," she said matter-of-factly.

That waitress perfectly summed up the attitude a company should have toward its products. When a product satisfies enough customers that it makes money for the company, the product is a winner. If, on the other hand, a product doesn't make money, there is no reason to produce it—even if some customers are disappointed.

Fear of change, laziness, and an overattachment to tradition are not going to keep your company viable. Satisfying customers and making a profit, in that order, are ultimately the only good reasons for a product's continued existence.

QUALITY MEASUREMENTS

Answer all customer and employee comments and suggestions promptly. Review these with the senior management committee to determine whether product or people implications are broader than one event. Review on-time data, fare levels, service levels, waiting time—and take action to be competitive. Take in-flight customer surveys twice a year.

In order to ensure consistently high-quality service, a company must be concerned with and sensitive to the perceptions of its customers. Basically, an executive needs to ask the question that one former big-city mayor would regularly pose to his constituency: "How'm I doin'?"

This seemingly simple question is one that is extremely difficult to answer objectively. With quality measurements, a company must contend with perceptions, feelings, and opinions—all subjective assessments. Nevertheless, you can get the answers you need if you take the time to listen.

Executives and managers need to pay attention to what their employees and customers are trying to tell them. Listening is an active process that implicitly requires an appropriate response on the part of the listener.

To listen effectively, executives need only open their ears and begin taking an active part in conversations with employees and customers. If you want to know what's going on, ask questions and be sensitive to what you are told.

Make time in your busy schedule to talk with your customers and employees. If you pay careful attention to what they're telling you, it will be time well spent. Listen for trends in their positive and negative responses to products, policies, and procedures. Concentrate on dealing with those trends—and the isolated incidents will take care of themselves.

Remember, poor quality and poor service are symptomatic of problems somewhere in your strategy. The key to locating those problems is becoming a good listener. Then, when you pinpoint the trouble spots, you will be well on your way to determining the best way to proceed.

6

The $27,000 Cocktail: Contain Costs—At All Costs

About two weeks after Phil Guthrie and I arrived at Braniff, I was sitting at my desk on a Tuesday morning. Suddenly, Phil charged into my office, madder than I had ever seen him.

"What do you make of this?" he snapped, as he threw an invoice on my desk. It was from a fancy New York restaurant called Tavern on the Green, and the bottom line of that invoice was $27,000—which represented the food and drink tab for one night's worth of entertaining customers. The expenditure had been approved by our then–vice president of sales.

Just two weeks earlier, I had called my first meeting with all officers and senior managers and expressed my concern over Braniff's current situation, its severe cash crunch, and how little time we had to turn things around. I expounded a bit on my philosophy about productivity and financial planning—and was glad to see most of the officers nodding in agreement. They all seemed thankful that someone had finally come on board to lead them out of a financial crisis that posed an immediate threat to the airline's future.

Before the meeting ended, everyone stated their commitment

to the new way of doing things. They all said that, as soon as they returned to their offices, they would start cutting back on expenses and costs. I felt good that my words had such an immediate impact.

But obviously there had been a gap in communications somewhere along the line. Confused as well as angry, I immediately went to the office of the vice president who authorized the $27,000 expenditure and demanded an explanation. "Why did we spend this $27,000?" I asked.

"Well, we've done it every year," he answered.

"Can you measure the results of such a hefty expenditure?"

"Uh, not really."

"So why did we spend $27,000 when less than two weeks ago we talked about how cash short we were? Do you remember that discussion?"

"Oh, yes, of course. I certainly understand how important it is for us to cut back everywhere we can."

"Okay, then why did you spend this $27,000?" By this time, my anger and frustration couldn't have been more apparent.

"Because we've always done it," the vice president answered, "and the preplanned expense was in my budget."

Unnecessary expenses like this are common occurrences at many companies. They are the direct result of the typical budgeting mentality that creates untold waste. There is a pervasive feeling that goes like this: "I'd better spend what I have in this year's budget. If I don't, they won't think I need so much money, and they'll give me even less next year."

Shortly after the $27,000 invoice was brought to my attention, Phil Guthrie and I took steps to ensure that this would not happen again—we eliminated budgets completely. No one had the authority to spend money on anything—be it fuel, advertising, pencils, or whatever—without our approval.

Budgets are systems, and systems generate behaviors and attitudes that don't necessarily reflect a company's needs. If your systems are out of line, your people will respond accordingly. The way we dealt with this problem at Braniff was to change those systems immediately—particularly with respect to costs. We accomplished this with the following ten-part plan, which you can adapt to suit your own company's needs.

Create a Living Plan That Emanates from the Top

A plan is dead the minute it is committed to paper. Think about it: whatever you write down at a given time can reflect only the forces that affect your business at that moment. For better or worse, your company's market position—indeed, its entire economic outlook—is subject to constant change. Here are some things that can happen even as you read these words:

- A major Japanese conglomerate decides to enter your industry.
- The stock market crashes (again).
- A war breaks out, and the whole economy is turned on its ear.
- Your ever-fickle consumers make your product the new vogue.
- A huge new source of raw material is discovered.
- It is announced that an ingredient in your product prevents (or causes) cancer.

A company's leaders must be prepared for such eventualities. In order to create a true living plan, they must stay current with economic and other changes on which their organization's fortunes can turn. These include shifts in gross national product, industry projections, real and anticipated moves by the competition, consumer buying trends, and interest rates.

During my tenure at Southwest we constantly looked at all these factors. In the three years I was there, we had three splits of the common stock and three equity offerings, all of which occurred in concert with the opportunities brought about by deregulation. The company's after-tax profits during this period were a healthy 10 percent. This was accomplished through cohesive and comprehensive top-down planning—a process that actively involved every senior manager in structuring the company's financial, investment, profitability, and strategic plans.

It is critical that the CEO and the senior management team work together in setting the financial, investment, and profitability goals for the entire organization. These goals should be long term, wide ranging, and far reaching. Each must be linked to the strategic plan in an achievable manner. If properly conceived and executed, a company's goals take on a superordinate quality and thus become the stars that guide it through both calm and turbulent waters.

At Southwest, senior management stayed actively involved in the corporate financial planning process from the beginning. Phil Guthrie, the CFO, and I would have one all-day session where we reviewed all available information about the economy, the competition, and anything else we felt could have an impact on our business. Then we set tentative goals—asking for input from the other officers.

Each officer shared his or her view about whether the goals were obtainable and then discussed the goals until we had a set that everyone felt was attainable. At that point, I'd present the entire package to the board for approval, and we'd start to put our plan into action.

The senior management team met regularly to ensure that our plan was responsive to ever-changing conditions. Each officer discussed the performance of his or her department and presented relevant financial statistics. I encouraged my officers to have frank discussions with our CFO. Through these regular meetings and informal talks, the plan was kept alive in our thoughts and actions.

As an additional reminder, each of us carried a small pocket trifold that contained all relevant long- and short-term financial information. This written summary of our plan and updated results was revised monthly.

The essence of the plan was filtered down to all employees through word of mouth, written memos, and interdepartmental meetings so that they could do their part in implementing the company's goals. Our overriding financial philosophy maintained that whoever had control over something was accountable for it. This gave middle managers a sense of involvement and responsibility. Still, everyone in the company knew that the ultimate responsibility for conceiving and revising the plan rested with the senior management team.

The kind of financial plan we put into place at Southwest was alive in every sense of the word. It was alive in the thoughts and actions of our senior and middle managers—as well as our front-line people. Our financial plan was also alive in the market-place—because it was constantly responding and adapting to changes in the environment.

A living plan requires great managerial skill, regular and careful thought, and decisive action. It's not necessarily the easiest approach to spending. But although other ways may involve less effort, none is as productive, efficient, or empowering to those who use it.

Remain Flexible and Utilize Frequent Forecasts

I find it helpful to compare a company's financial plan to the needs of a living organism. Just as an animal or human being is susceptible to changes in its environment, a business is susceptible to changes in the marketplace. As human beings, one of the things we must plan for is the consumption of food, without which we would die. To meet that need each day, many of us have a basic plan for when and where we are going to eat—and how much we are going to consume. Nevertheless, we must remain flexible.

Consider this: Your basic eating plan is built around three meals a day: breakfast is eaten at home, lunch in the office or at a restaurant with a client, and dinner normally at home. Once a week, you and your spouse eat dinner in a restaurant, and occasionally you have dinner out with a client or business associate.

You've thought through your plan in terms of nutrition, comfort, and expense. You've even put it down on paper—allowing for a certain amount of flexibility. If, for example, you have a big lunch out with a client at an expensive restaurant, you try to follow that up with a light dinner at home. Most of the time, your environment remains sufficiently stable for you to stick with your plan. But suddenly, a number of unforeseen events take place.

One night there is a power failure, and by morning, the milk has gone sour and the toaster doesn't work. You ate the last doughnut in the house before going to bed, and you can't make coffee in your electric percolator. As a result, you eat breakfast out. That same day, two different clients insist on having lunch out with you at two separate times. You can't say no to either, so you wind up eating lunch twice: once at noon, and a second time at 2 P.M.

Just as you are heading home, looking forward to a quiet dinner, the manager of your department calls you into her office to congratulate you on the marvelous job you have been doing. She'd like to take you to her favorite restaurant tonight and talk about her plans to expand your responsibilities. She says she'll understand if you can't make it, but you are hard pressed not to accept her offer.

How would you respond to these kinds of changes in your environment? Would you become disoriented and develop an upset stomach because you felt you were losing control, or would you smoothly adapt to these unexpected occurrences?

A plan is nothing more than a guide for action within an arena that is constantly changing. The demands of the environment must drive actions. The purpose of a plan is to reflect those demands, and frequent forecasting is crucial. Only by constantly evaluating the environment within which we do business and anticipating changes can we survive and thrive.

During one Christmas season while I was at Southwest, we noted that retail sales had dipped far below expectations. Further research showed a softness in the consumer purchase of capital goods, which translated into softer discretionary spending for air travel and reduced revenue for us.

As we saw it, the question was not whether it was necessary to institute changes: it was clear that something needed to be done, and our living plan required us to adapt to our environment. The question was, do we lower fares and try to stimulate business while keeping the plant the same size, or do we cut the size of the plant?

We elected to cut the size of our plant: we canceled 10 percent of our flights for sixty days, saving fuel, labor, and maintenance costs. In addition, we offered employees additional time off—without pay. Because it was the holiday season, a number of people took advantage of this opportunity.

This immediately reduced our operating costs by another 6 percent—without causing a measurable drop in revenues and profitability.

Our original plan had called for us to do a certain amount of business in January and February, but the customers just weren't there. Instead of riding out a plan that no longer reflected our needs, we changed it. Our flexibility minimized the harm of this unforeseen change in the market. In March, when business began to pick up, we were ready. Frequent forecasting allowed us to quickly size down and size back up again.

In drawing up your company's plans, remember that they are not supposed to be a granite monument—but a flexible guide for action in an ever-changing marketplace.

Stress Quality and Customer Service Rather Than the Bottom Line

My experience has been that quality and efficiency breed profit. That's why we put quality and service measures ahead of profit measures. Naturally we maintained a healthy concern with profitability, but the actions and attitudes of the people at Southwest were rooted in service and quality rather than the bottom line.

I believe that if you do what you are doing with the utmost quality and the highest regard for the customer, the bottom line will almost always take care of itself—assuming there is a market for your product or service.

At Southwest, we recorded the number of customer complaints per 100,000 passengers in varying categories, such as bags mishandled and flights canceled. We also measured our on-time performance, our aircraft on-the-ground turnaround time, and the quality of our in-flight service. These measurements helped us set service goals that reduced the number of complaints.

This emphasis on service and quality was reflected in increased profits for the airline.

At Southwest, we strived to answer the phone within twenty seconds 90 percent of the time. That service goal immediately translated into how many reservation agents had to be on the payroll to accommodate current and anticipated calls. That, in turn, helped determine this portion of our top-down living plan.

In setting similar goals for your company, your financial plan may not support the level of service you are trying to achieve. In that case, you may have to drop your service level to, say, 80 percent of the calls to be answered within twenty seconds. These things vary from industry to industry. But whatever your business, your company's service goals must always be in line with its resources and financial objectives.

I have seen too many businesses increase their service goals even though they lack the necessary cash flow or reserves to make those goals a reality. Without a balance between product quality, customer service, and cash flow, a business will stumble and eventually fall.

Utilize Productivity Goals Instead of Budgets

Whenever I talk about doing away with budgets, people seem to become confused. "What else am I going to use as a guide for spending?" they ask. My response can be summed up in two words—productivity goals.

People who are driven by productivity goals instead of budgets are concerned with how much they are accomplishing and not how much or how little they are spending. Of course financial planning is important. Still, I've watched too many companies court trouble by depending on budgets to guide their actions.

At Southwest, we stressed the productive utilization of our people and capital equipment in trying to realize our objectives. One of our main productivity goals was the number of passengers boarded per employee. We worked as a team to forge some challenging but realistic expectations for our people to meet. Then, the senior management team translated those findings into a dollar figure and allocated funds as they were needed.

In planning to meet this goal, we did not create a set budget, nor were there any automatic expenditures. Thirty days after a particular part of the plan was launched, we met to review whether that aspect of the program was still necessary and within our means. At no time was there ever a license to spend.

Large bureaucratic companies typically approve expenditures for an entire year. That's far too long a time frame considering the kind of economic climate in which we now have to operate. For many years, Delta has gone to the opposite extreme. It mandates that all expenditures be approved on a weekly basis—down to desks, typewriters, reams of paper, and pencils.

Although we were not that diligent at Southwest, we were strict about spending. Hard experience taught us never to assume a stable, unchanging environment.

One of my main problems with budgets is that they are notoriously bad for making realistic projections. Furthermore, the entire budgeting process, as practiced in most bureaucratic companies, takes far too much time.

When I was at United Airlines, for example, the process of budgeting consumed over 10 percent of our annual time—deterring us from productive and revenue-generating activities. By comparison, the living, productivity-based plan we implemented at Southwest took up less than 4 percent of our annual time. One reason for this discrepancy was that we benefited from having a flat organization.

In the bottom-up budget planning of many large corporations, things tend to stall as they move from level to bureaucratic level. Decisions made at a lower level are reviewed and then sent back down the line. At that point, those same issues are reviewed once again—and then sent back on their way to the top.

By the time the process is complete, an inordinate amount of time been taken to accomplish the allocation of funds. Moreover, the final figures can be bloated by as much as 45 percent. I have found that as budgets pass through each organizational level, there is a tendency to add anywhere from 3 to 5 percent in padding.

People at each level fear that if they don't overestimate, they will be budgeted fewer dollars than what they need. To protect themselves, they add a certain amount of padding to whatever the real estimate is. Imagine what this adds up to in a ten-layer company and you'll recognize some of the inherent dangers of the traditional budgeting process.

Offer Your People Incentives That Are Consistent with Achievement

I strongly believe in profit sharing and ownership at every level. Beyond wanting a piece of the action, human beings have a strong need to collaborate with others in building something meaningful. A good business leader should never underestimate the importance of those needs and desires.

Southwest instituted a profit-sharing plan for every employee from the beginning of its existence. It included a quarterly cash payment if certain short-term corporate and departmental goals were achieved. That payment was the same for every employee— from the folks at the front line right up to the CEO.

For the achievement of annual goals, employees were rewarded by additional contributions to the profit-sharing plan in the form of stock and cash that fully vested after a ten-year period of employment. In addition, key officers and managers were remunerated with additional incentive plans for outstanding achievement. This was based, to a large extent, on my own subjective evaluations.

This example should give you a fuller understanding of how we structured our profit-sharing system at Southwest. Annual corporate goals during our tenure at the airline looked something like this:

Revenue	$240 million
Operating profit	$48 million
Accidents	0
Lost-time injuries	Not to exceed X per 20,000 hours worked
Customer complaints	Not to exceed X per 100,000 passengers boarded
Passengers boarded per employee	3,400
Utilization of each aircraft	11 hours per day
Break-even load factor	49%

In addition to these corporate goals, each senior officer and manager also had three or four department-specific goals, one of which usually entailed cost reduction in their particular area. I also emphasized the importance of my subjective judgments in determining additional rewards key managers and executives could receive for outstanding achievement. In making those determinations, I looked for a positive attitude, a willingness to show initiative, and an ability to make others feel as if they were part of the team. In any case, there would be no bonuses, salary increases, or profit-sharing incentives for anyone if the targeted corporate goals were not reached. Once those criteria were met, the monetary rewards started to click in.

The system we developed was simple and achievement oriented. It sent one message to everyone in the company. If you go the extra mile, you will be rewarded for your efforts. If you do only what is expected, the company will progress, but at a much slower rate, and you will not receive the same kind of additional rewards.

We also structured our incentive program so that most of the benefits started taking effect only after someone was with the company for three to five years. This helped keep our people committed and involved.

Through accountability and profit-sharing incentives, you can develop the kind of team spirit that underlies many successful companies. By rewarding individual achievement—and placing such achievement within a team context—you add strength that cannot be measured in dollars.

Insist on Timely and Candid Reporting

People like to report good news, and so do companies. Bad news can be taken as an indication of poor performance, and sometimes it is. Companies do not like to present bad news to stakeholders because it is often perceived to be the result of bad management—and sometimes that is where the problem lies. Still, facing up to bad news can be a key to positive change because it provides a fertile context for reassessment.

Markets may have shifted. Competition may have increased.

All sorts of adverse conditions may have presented themselves. In any case, not-so-happy reports should be taken in hand and used as tools for investigation—not as excuses for criticism and buck passing.

Problems can be sorted out more effectively when they are reported promptly and honestly. Delaying or glossing over bad news is always counterproductive. In the short run, you may cover your rear. But over the long haul, you are bound to lose credibility with your employees, your shareholders, and your customers—not to speak of the media and the public at large.

Phil Guthrie, board chairman Herb Kelleher, and I worked hard to keep the shareholders informed of our progress at Southwest, where the news was almost always good. When Phil and I moved to Braniff, we employed the same policy—even though the news was often bad to terrible. In either case, our approach was consistent.

I encouraged senior officials at both companies to discuss their departments' financial performance and statistics with Phil, with me—and with anyone else in the company. Sweeping unpleasant details under the rug was never tolerated.

Phil and I were always kept informed of what was going on in both companies. We made frequent and candid presentations and statements to our boards, to the media, and to the investment community. We encouraged visits to our facilities, so that our claims could be confirmed by anyone who cared to look. We made it our business to keep all stakeholders and other interested parties informed at all times.

Once or twice a year, Phil, Herb, and I traveled to Wall Street to inform the investment community of our status. We usually took with us a pilot, a flight attendant, and a reservation agent. Each of them gave a five-minute talk during our presentation, adding warmth and credibility to the proceedings.

I have found that one of the surest ways to avoid trouble in business is by insisting on timely and candid reporting that can be reviewed quickly. Massive documents written in highly technical language are so imposing and complex that nobody bothers to read them. Keep your reporting process simple, timely, and honest—and you will have forged one of the sharpest weapons a company can have in times of crisis.

Keep Your Accounting Systems
Simple, Succinct, and Up-to-date

While you're streamlining your reporting process, consider doing the same with your financial statements. To make quick and meaningful decisions, busy executives need accounting information that is concise and readily understandable. Huge runs of computer paper laden with vast numbers tend to gather dust—and deservedly so.

A company must generate financial information that executives and managers can readily scan on a daily, weekly, and monthly basis. This information must correlate with short- and long-term goals to be of real value. An officer simply cannot wait thirty days for a daily cost report or spend an entire afternoon trying to decipher it.

Install a Strong and Independent Chief
Financial Officer

Given today's economic environment, the chief financial officer may be the most important member of your senior management team. This person cannot be just a number cruncher. He or she must install effective and efficient accounting systems—but that is just the beginning. Ideally, your CFO should possess a keen sense of marketing and a feel for every aspect of your company's strategic plan. Phil Guthrie is just such a person.

When I met Phil, he was in his mid-thirties with a CPA from a small college in Louisiana and a master's degree from the University of Michigan. He had spent three years at Price Waterhouse in Houston and some time with a small venture-capital firm in Dallas. By the time our paths crossed, he had all the credentials I was looking for—the right kind of education as well as Big Eight and entrepreneurial experience. Phil also had the right attitude for the kind of corporate environment I wanted to create at Southwest.

I was looking for team members who were spirited and aggressive. At the time, Southwest was a young, entrepreneurial company that was on the verge of becoming a big regional player. I was brought in to help catapult the airline to that next level. Phil was young for a CFO, but his youth and enthusiasm were perfect for Southwest.

In addition to his professional qualifications, Phil was also a fine man. I have always made intuitive evaluations of the people with whom I work. Those gut-level judgments are important in helping me determine whether or not a person can get the job done. I knew that we needed some new blood in restructuring Southwest's finances, and Phil was the man.

When I became CEO of that airline, I had the sense that our cost-containment procedures left something to be desired. One of the first things I did was ask the then-controller how the company decided to buy its airplanes.

He leaned back in his chair, shot me a quizzical glance, and said, "Well, when we get enough money in the bank, we just go out and buy one."

So I asked him, "How do you know if you need it, and where you're going to use it?"

And he said, "We usually figure that out after we've placed the order."

Although Southwest was turning a profit, I was upset by this attitude toward planning and spending. I knew that no company could thrive—or even survive—for long under this kind of financial leadership. We were still in the Alpha state, but there were storm clouds on the horizon. We needed to be cognizant of them quickly, or soon Southwest could be in the Beta phase of turbulence described in Chapter 1. Southwest still had more than adequate cash flow, but there was no doubt in my mind that complacency would eventually catch up with it. That's why I immediately brought Phil Guthrie on board.

There are certain essential qualities that every CFO needs. He or she must be a strong and independent financial leader who can also function as part of a team. One of Phil's first tasks at Southwest was to put together a financial plan that was simple to understand—one that drew on the input of every member of the senior management team.

The plan Phil put together was generated top-down, so that we didn't waste a lot of time with bottom-up budgeting. He was an integral part of the success we achieved at Southwest—and of the restructuring we were able to effect at Braniff.

Phil proved just how talented he was by providing strong financial leadership in two companies that were at very different junctures in their respective histories. Southwest was in a growth mode; Braniff on the verge of complete collapse. In both instances, Phil was able to furnish the kind of skill and leadership that was needed to achieve positive results. Your company's fortunes are subject to change in a hurry, and your CFO must be capable of being a strong leader in both good and bad times.

Avoid Too Much Leverage

Companies are often eager to grow out of their niche before they have the means. Instead of concentrating on what they do best, these companies expand by increasing their debt-to-equity ratio. Because of the unpredictable and cyclical nature of our economy, this kind of speculation can ultimately catch up with and sometimes crush a company. Evidence is mounting that the leveraged buyouts of the 1980s will cause pain and suffering through the 1990s and beyond.

Given today's volatile markets, few companies can rely on the sale of assets to save them in lean times. If the equity market wants to invest in your young company now, remember that it is easier to raise money when you don't need it and others have it than when the tables are turned.

Keep Operating Costs Down

I strongly believe in minimizing costs in both good and bad times. At both Southwest and Braniff, I did what I could to keep costs down. In one case, I dealt with a crisis; in the other, I intentionally adopted a crisis-like approach to ensure the company's continued success.

As I mentioned in the discussion of incentives, each department manager at Southwest was responsible for cost reduction in a specific departmental area. Normally, such a measure is instituted when a company experiences a financial downturn. But I felt it was important to employ this and other thrift measures—even though some people felt that our financial status did not warrant such steps.

One of the keys to Southwest's prosperity was its success at keeping costs nearly 50 percent below the industry standard. The airline industry utilizes a measurement of cost per available seat mile. Southwest's cost was five cents, while the rest of the industry was at eight to nine cents. Rather than taking the attitude that we could relax and be a little less frugal, we continued to run the company as if our good fortunes could turn around at any second—which, of course, they could.

When Phil and I arrived at Braniff, the crisis was real. The company was on the brink of bankruptcy, and drastic cost-cutting measures had to be taken.

One of our first targets was Braniff's elaborate headquarters building. It was an outlandish example of unnecessary and lavish spending. The facility was a modern, three-story building of almost 500,000 square feet. There was an apartment for then-chairman Harding Lawrence, equipped with its own swimming pool. Attached to the headquarters building was a 100-room hotel for housing layover crews who were there for training. This included an exercise facility complete with an Olympic-size swimming pool, a bowling alley, a nine-hole golf course, and a baseball diamond.

The cost on the lease alone was over a half million dollars a month, not including maintenance and utilities—a bit excessive for a company that was fighting for its life. On our arrival at Braniff, I announced that the building was for lease and that we would be moving into the first available warehouse.

This gesture sent an important message to employees, lenders, and the public at large: we were going to eliminate nonessential overhead. In a crisis situation, you must start cutting anywhere and everywhere that you see fat. You can't afford to be sentimental.

At Braniff, we had a collection of paintings by Alexander Calder. They were the only works of art allowed to hang at corporate headquarters. We put the collection up for sale immediately. This was another signal that tradition and a business-as-usual attitude were no longer acceptable. Corporate art is a luxury item that should not be purchased or owned at the expense of operating a healthy business.

When a company is in crisis, its leaders must eliminate the superfluous and get back to basics. That means cutting out all products that are losing money. When we arrived at Braniff, we discovered that our new Canadian routes were losing almost three-quarters of a million dollars a month. These were immediately eliminated. We also got rid of product lines that were not making a positive cash contribution.

Whether your company is thriving or struggling, I strongly suggest that you immediately take steps to cut fat wherever you can. And don't procrastinate: things seldom get better on their own. You have to make it happen!

When evaluating the financial state of your company, start out by looking for the $27,000 parties, the Olympic swimming pools, and the expensive fine art collections. After those things are trimmed, look for the smaller, less obvious costs that accumulate and eventually get out of control.

Beyond any specific measures, it is essential that you encourage an attitude of thrift among your people and support it with action that emanates from the top. It is also essential that you keep your approach simple: the simpler, the better. A simple approach includes a simplified strategy, simplified plans, and simplified systems to execute those plans. This trimmed-down approach will result in simplified costs—which are much easier to keep track of and contain.

*   *   *

In closing this section on cost containment and alternatives to the traditional budgeting process, I am reminded of a conversation I had with a man named Don Ogden shortly after I arrived at Southwest.

Don was vice president of flight, in charge of pilots. Some years before, he had retired from American Airlines as a captain on

707s. Captain O, as everyone called him, was a wonderful guy of about sixty-eight who always had a pipe in his mouth. My first conversation with Don concerned the financial status of his department.

"Don," I said, "let me see your budget."

"Howard," Captain O responded in a slow Texas drawl, as he leaned back in his chair and blew a big puff of pipe smoke. "We don't have a budget: we only spend money when we have to."

That one sentence pretty well sums up my feelings about budgets and the attitude a company needs to keep its costs under control.

7

Are We Having Fun Yet?
It Takes More Than Just a
Paycheck

When I was twenty-one I worked for Capital Airlines. In that year, I moved from adolescence to adulthood. During the previous three years, I also had moved from baggage handler to passenger-service manager to sales representative at Capital. When I moved up to sales, I also moved from Midway Airport to the downtown Chicago office—where I found myself in a department headed by Dick Marasco.

Dick—a senior salesperson on the cargo side—was well known for his racy sense of humor. He was a big guy who always walked around with a loose tie and a half-empty cup of coffee in his hand. Whenever you happened into Dick's office, he'd be sitting with his size-twelve feet propped up on his desk. He always had a glimmer in his eye—one that betrayed him as the kind of guy who was forever thinking of new ways to rattle people. This particular time, the target of Dick's humor was Barbara, his secretary.

One September, Dick decided to throw a contest for his freight customers. He called it the Most Risqué Story of the Month Contest. The person who could create the most vividly detailed carnal episode would receive a bottle of expensive French champagne.

As Dick's secretary, it was Barbara's job to open his mail—including the sealed envelopes containing the risqué writings. I was the new kid in the office, but Barbara came to me with her plight.

"Howard," she said, almost in tears. "I've had just about all I can take. I know I'm his secretary, but do I have to read all these lewd stories?"

"No," I replied. "I guess you don't."

"But what can I do? It's part of my job to screen Dick's mail. I have to open all the envelopes, so I can't avoid getting a glimpse before I pass it on to him. Some of the stuff I've read is really raunchy."

"I'll tell you what, Barbara," I said, with a mischievous glimmer in my eye. "Let's have a little fun with ol' Dick. Get a plain white sheet of paper without the corporate name on it, and I'll dictate a letter to you."

Barbara wasn't sure what I had in mind, but she obliged. I then proceeded to concoct a letter from a fictitious U.S. postal inspector named MacIntosh. The letter informed Dick that, because he used the U.S. Postal Service for the interstate movement of pornographic materials, he was in violation of section so and so, paragraph so and so, of the U.S. Postal Code. The letter further stated if he did not cease and desist, serious penalties might occur—possibly even a jail sentence.

Barbara and I mailed the letter immediately, and it arrived back at the office the following day. Barbara opened it and placed it on Dick's desk—right on top of the stack of off-color stories he had received that day. Twenty minutes later, my phone rang. It was Barbara, and she sounded even more desperate than when she first approached me about the contest:

"Howard, our little joke backfired. Dick got really concerned when he read the letter, and he called the U.S. Postal Department. It turns out that there really is a postal inspector named MacIntosh. He and Dick just got off the phone. I listened to the call, and Dick was apologizing profusely. The inspector didn't know what was going on, but he was definitely curious about what kind of violations Dick was talking about. He probably figured that there must be something pretty serious going on for him to call up apologizing like this."

Barbara paused to catch her breath. Then she continued, almost in tears: "I didn't want to let things go any further. So I wrote Dick a note explaining that the whole thing was all a joke—and that it was your idea. I just ran into his office while he was on the phone, and I held the note in front of his face." There was a pregnant pause.

"And—" I said sheepishly, anticipating what was coming next.

"And," Barbara responded, "Dick got real mad, Howard. He's heading your way right now."

I won't quote what Dick said when he caught up to me. Suffice it to say that I nearly got fired for that one. The new kid had no business trying to put one over on the likes of Dick Marasco. Luckily, the spirit of the joke spread quickly and everyone laughed. After a while, even Dick laughed—although it took him a little longer to see the humor in the situation.

Over the years, I have found that humor is a powerful tie between the people who work at a company. A good time is infectious: a fun atmosphere bonds employees to one another and links them to the organization in a positive way.

My philosophy about having fun in the workplace can be summed up as follows: take your job seriously, but always keep a sense of humor about yourself.

For this philosophy to be most effective, it must come from a company's leader and radiate throughout the organization. When humor emanates from a company's CEO, it can have a snowball effect—picking up new people and departments as it rolls along.

A smile as you walk through the office in the morning can start the ball rolling. Simple gestures can set the tone for the entire day. When, on the other hand, a leader appears to be unhappy, frustrated, or bored, this display of negativity can also have a ripple effect throughout the company.

People don't often think about it in this light, but happiness is one of the inalienable rights granted to us by the founders of this country. Life, liberty, and the pursuit of happiness are written into the United States' Declaration of Independence. Apparently our forefathers felt that elevation of the human spirit was an important enough goal to include as part of our nation's guiding principles.

Since work is such an important part of most Americans' lives, companies have an obligation to address their employees' right to find a degree of happiness on the job. There are, in fact, practical reasons for a company to create a positive and happy atmosphere: if people are not happy on the job, they will quit and go elsewhere—or they'll stay and give less than their best efforts.

During my four decades as an employee, executive, and consultant, I have seen how fun can reduce the negative energy that is a common by-product of the day-to-day tensions of doing business. A fun atmosphere reduces stress and its related health problems. This translates into fewer days lost due to illness.

People who enjoy going to work invariably make bigger and better contributions to a company's success. When employees are happy, there tends to be less petty bickering and theft. A feeling of joy and shared laughter makes people feel loyal and committed to an organization, and this kind of positive atmosphere almost always translates into increased productivity and profitability.

Fun also can affect a company's image and reputation in the marketplace. It should not be thought of as a panacea, but fun can be an important facet of a successful enterprise. Think about the valuable human dimension fun adds to the work experience. It can be even more satisfying than increased paychecks and promotions.

How to Get the Ball Rolling

A company's commitment to fun is not about joke-telling CEOs or most-risqué-story contests. It is an attitude that pervades the company's actions. It begins before an employee is hired, continues even after he or she retires—and influences everything that takes place in between.

Fun is more than just a good joke or an occasional laugh. When I use the term *fun* to describe the atmosphere in a company, I am talking about a pervasive spirit that encompasses an organization's ability to think positively—even to laugh at itself. That spirit becomes an essential part of an organization's public image. It is expressed in a company's optimism when it faces challenging and difficult situations and in the enthusiasm with which it serves its customers.

To me, a fun organization is one whose culture allows responsibility and enjoyment to synergize and empower each other. Employees and customers can sense that spirit in every aspect of the way an organization is run. It is revealed by how various jobs are described and by the kind of people hired to fill those jobs. The spirit of a company is reflected in the kind of procedures and policies it uses to manage its people. And, like every other important aspect of a business's operation, the spirit of fun must emanate from the top.

I have always enjoyed a good laugh, it's part of my nature. I would have denied a piece of myself if I did not bring my appreciation of humor to the companies I have led.

If you are a business leader and humor is part of your nature, I urge you to utilize this valuable resource to your company's best advantage. Use this positive form of communication to lighten the mood and lift the spirit of everyone with whom you come in contact. If you believe that humor is not part of your nature, try to loosen up, and you'll see it start to surface.

I believe that the ability to laugh and have fun is alive in all of us. Even if you choose not to develop this quality, you must, for the sake of your employees and your customers, find a way to make it an integral part of your organization.

In order to create a spirit of fun, you must attract the right people—men and women who engender a good-time atmosphere. Once you hire them, you must then match them with the right positions and the right leadership and help them stay motivated and happy.

The Process of Attraction

The founders of Southwest made it a point to instill a spirit of fun into its operation. The fun at Southwest started with the uniform worn by the flight attendants—shorts and boots. It continued with free drinks during the day—and the company's emphasis on the concept of love.

Since Southwest was headquartered at Love Field in Dallas, it used the word *love* wherever possible in its public relations activities. For example, the company's musical theme was called

"Spreading Love through Texas." During flights, Southwest served peanuts called "love bites." This approach was part of an overall philosophy of creating a fun atmosphere for both employees and customers.

United's general philosophy did not include fun, so I was particularly refreshed by the lighthearted spirit I found at Southwest. I also could not help but notice that, along with the fun atmosphere, there was commitment and dedication. I looked forward to continuing and expanding the tradition of fun at Southwest.

When I flew Southwest or when I walked through the Southwest terminal at Love Field, I was struck by the quality of the people. The flight attendants and ticket agents had extraordinary attitudes. Each day they handled missed connections, delayed flights, language barriers, crying babies, lost tickets, and testy customers who insisted on carrying baggage on board that could not fit. Yet rarely did these people lose their positive attitude.

I watched these women and men negotiate one difficult situation after another without showing signs of stress or frustration. There were exceptions, of course, but, in general, the dispositions of the front-line employees at Southwest were completely different from the dispositions of their counterparts at United. The job titles and responsibilities were virtually the same at both airlines. Where, then, did the difference lie?

While flight attendants at both airlines had to accomplish the same tasks, they had very different views of their jobs.

At a graduation ceremony for Southwest flight attendants, I asked for all those who were cheerleaders, twirlers, boosters, or majorettes in high school or college to raise their hands. About 70 percent of the graduates fit into one or more of those categories. At that ceremony I realized how influential a job description can be in determining the kind of person who is attracted to a particular position.

I'm convinced that the uniform was a big reason that Southwest had so many energetic, outgoing, enthusiastic, and friendly women working as flight attendants and ticket agents. Many of the women who applied for the job wanted to wear the uniform because it was, in some way, an extension of activities they had enjoyed in school. Some women had no desire to wear shorts, and others may have been offended by the idea. If so, they could choose to work at a number of other airlines that had more traditional dress codes for their flight attendants.

There was, of course, far more to the Southwest flight attendant's job description than what she wore. Nevertheless, it is clear that the Southwest uniform attracted a certain type of individual to the organization—a woman who felt good about herself. Someone who enjoyed wearing shorts and boots tended to be outgoing and optimistic. She never felt as if she were meeting a stranger, and the casualness of her attire seemed to make customers—female as well as male—feel at ease. Southwest did away with the uniform in the early 1980s, but the spirit of fun that the uniform symbolized remains in its employees to this day.

This kind of foresight in planning contributes to the building of a happy organization. A company can use something as simple as a certain kind of clothing to attract the kind of personalities it wants to its organization. Usually, however, recruitment issues are far more subtle and complex. A company can draw the right people by using any area of the work experience—including incentives, scheduling, training, recognition, and opportunity. A public job description might read, "One day per month, as an employee of this company, you will have the opportunity to work in another department in a comparable position. You will have the chance to learn and to grow and to determine whether you might be better suited or happier in another area of the company."

A company that is aware of the value of attracting the right people would never use this job description: "Data-entry position, 9 to 5, Monday through Friday, $7.00 per hour."

Even entry-level positions should have detailed job descriptions—the kind that entice individuals who are likely to stay and advance within a company. Every company can describe a job in such a way as to interest a well-suited personality. Every company should seize that opportunity, especially for front-line positions where customer interaction is critical.

If a company wants quality-minded, highly productive people, the job description must include competitive wages and incentives. If a company wants innovative people, the job description must include rewards for coming up with new ideas. If a company wants proud, confident people, the job description must include recognition for achievement. If a company wants responsible people, the job description must include accountability. Finally, if a company wants people who enjoy serving the customer, the job description must emphasize interpersonal skills.

People who are well suited for their jobs are far happier—and therefore more productive—than those who are not. Happy employees reflect a company's positive outlook. The organization that recognizes how important this is to its future can develop job descriptions that correspond to its goals.

Many companies develop job descriptions that are too technical and do not depict the job in human terms. As a result, the most desirable people may turn elsewhere.

I find that experience and educational standards for many jobs are higher than necessary. A company with a pool of overqualified individuals—men and women who quickly become bored and unhappy—faces negative consequences in terms of productivity and the bottom line. It's a good idea to review your job qualifications and see whether they reflect your current needs.

Several years ago, a major airline required at least two years of college education for its reservations agents. This made sense before the widespread use of computers in the airline business, when a reservations agent's job required decision-making responsibilities. Once the tasks were computerized, however, the job needed different skills and traits.

Today, a reservations agent is basically a conduit for information between a customer and the airline. The job's main task is data entry, which requires patience and good phone skills as well as a tolerance for heavy eyestrain and minimal physical movement. At this point, college-level skills are no longer necessary— or even desirable.

The airline eliminated the college education requirement. Management understood that overqualified applicants would quickly grow bored and frustrated sitting at a computer terminal and typing all day, so they started looking for a different type of person.

Whenever I talk about the importance of structuring a job description to attract people who will be happy and motivated,

La Quinta Motor Inns comes to mind. Sam Barshop, the founder of that company, began with the premise that a motor inn is best run by a husband and wife—a family team that treats the inn like a home with a lot of bedrooms.

Armed with this job description, Barshop proceeded to look for couples in their fifties or sixties who wanted second careers. He designed the company to attract such couples. As managers of the company-owned inns, the husbands and wives lived at the motel, usually with the wife running the front desk and the husband handling maintenance and related responsibilities.

La Quinta has prospered with this kind of arrangement. In fact, Sam Barshop is more enthusiastic about the concept now than he was when the company was first created.

La Quinta was founded in San Antonio, Texas, in the early 1970s. Originally, the supply of husband-and-wife teams came from Lackland Air Force base, outside that city. The concept attracted career officers or enlisted men who were old enough to retire but still young enough for a second career. These former soldiers and their wives often had grown children who had left the nest. Managing a La Quinta Motor Inn gave such couples an activity they could pursue together in their later years.

Today, in response to the company's steady expansion, husband-wife teams are hired regionally, which gives them an opportunity to stay near their homes and families. Sam is proud of his success at attracting exactly the right people to manage these inns.

As with La Quinta, the success of any company has a great deal to do with the men and women who work for it—and good jobs attract good people.

All companies use some kind of conscious and unconscious process to draw people into the organization. Unfortunately, they often lack any particular design or long-term vision. When a company's attraction process evolves by default, the results are bound to be less than optimal. Until a company makes a conscious, well-considered decision about the kind of men and women it wants, it will inadvertently hire neutral people who are picking up a paycheck. You want to find people who are actively interested in and happy to be working for your company.

I believe that any job can attract good people. Every job is much more than merely a task or series of tasks that need completion. A job is a holistic experience that includes the following:

- Interaction with the culture of that company
- The working environment
- The potential for self-awareness, self-improvement, and self-actualization

As you have seen, a company has a good deal of control over the kind of people it attracts. The process starts with an appropriate job description that is reflected in the way help-wanted advertisements are worded and the way the interview process is conducted. Once a person is hired, an organization must make sure that the match between the new employee and company is empowering.

The needs of the individual and those of the organization must be satisfied simultaneously—not simply through the task at hand but through the entire job experience.

Matchmaker, Matchmaker, Make Us a Match

There are two levels on which a person is matched to a company. First, the individual must have the necessary skills to do the job. I call this the skills fit. Second, an individual must be matched with his or her leader and with other employees—that is, with the culture of the company. I call this the environmental fit.

Experience and education—the kind of information found on resumés—determine the skills fit. Personality, values, cultural background, and non–work-related interests—the kind of information unearthed during the interview process—determine the environmental fit. The skills fit establishes whether or not an individual can perform up to expectations. The environmental fit establishes whether he or she can perform better at one company or another. A good example of two companies that require similar skills but offer very different environments are Apple Computer and IBM.

Apple, in its early days, was a creative and relatively unstructured corporation. Its rules and policymaking were secondary to its development and marketing. IBM, on the other hand, was a disciplined and highly structured company that rewarded loyalty and strict adherence to policies and procedures. The skills required for comparable jobs at Apple and IBM were virtually the same, yet the cultures were almost totally dissimilar. A given individual might thrive in one environment and be miserable in the other.

Those doing the hiring in any company must recognize the nature of the work experience and the kind of person who is most likely to be comfortable and productive in that kind of environment.

When I hire an individual, I'm after compatibility, not just coexistence. That's why I look at the whole person. First I review the person's background and accomplishments in order to evaluate the skills. This makes up about 65 percent of my evaluation. The remaining 35 percent is determined by the environmental fit. To a great extent, this part of the process is subjective.

In determining the environmental fit, I look at the person's values and personality. If someone does not qualify in both those areas, he or she is not the right individual for the job. This is sometimes a tough decision to make—especially when the person scores high in terms of skills fit. Ultimately, I have to ask myself, "Will the two entities, individual and company, empower each other?" I believe that the ability to make this kind of tough, close call is one of the biggest challenges of leadership.

Shortly after my arrival at Southwest, we started searching for a chief financial officer. After interviewing several candidates without finding a complete fit, I met Phil Guthrie. He was thirty-two, shy and soft-spoken.

As I've mentioned elsewhere, Phil was a CPA and held a master's degree. He had worked with a public accounting firm and later served as vice president of manufacturing and finance for a start-up venture-capital company. Phil lacked airline experience, and I felt that his skill at managing people needed some development. Nevertheless, his education and track record made Phil a good skills fit—although not necessarily better than several other candidates I had interviewed.

Like me, Phil had grown up in a small town. As we talked, I discovered that we shared similar values. Openness, honesty, and integrity were as important to him as they were to me. Southwest was an energetic young company, and Phil was an enthusiastic young man—so the environmental match was certainly right in that respect.

The CFO for a company in transition needs to wear many hats. Phil's career thus far had given him a range of experience that was broader than finance. When I interviewed him, I learned of Phil's interest in all aspects of business. In the final analysis, Phil's superior environmental fit coupled with his comparable skills fit made him the best candidate. That's why I hired him as Southwest's CFO.

Phil and I worked well together at Southwest. When the Braniff opportunity presented itself, we moved to that airline together. After three years of running Southwest and improving its fortunes, we felt that our collective skills would be up to the task of meeting the considerable challenge of saving and restructuring a failing airline. It wasn't easy for us to leave the happy environment at Southwest to board a faltering ship, but we both welcomed the challenge. To put it another way, we felt well matched to the venture.

I believe that most people are intrinsically motivated to do a good job—given the right balance between challenge, contribution, and achievement. Many friends and associates thought I was crazy to leave a smooth operation like Southwest for a floundering organization like Braniff. Admittedly, the remuneration was somewhat better, but I would not have made the move if I did not welcome the challenge.

Each of us has a different comfort level in terms of the amount of challenge we consider desirable. A good leader understands that some employees simply don't want to tackle the challenge of increased responsibilities and decision making. Others feel uncomfortable with frequent promotions or advanced training. Senior management needs to recognize these differences and respond accordingly. This can be done by creating some positions that offer challenge and opportunity and others that offer stability and security.

Attracting and matching are not new methods of selecting

employees. Like many other principles that underlie successful business management, they are based largely on common sense. Unfortunately, however, these processes are often conducted in a haphazard and ineffective manner. To find the right kind of people, a company must actively use attraction and matching in its hiring practices. These are two of the most important steps in creating a motivated workforce—and a company that is a happy and fun place to work.

Spontaneous Fun

The most enjoyable experiences in a company are often un-planned. In many cases, they come from the spontaneous energy of people. Some of the best times we had at Southwest were rooted in casual suggestions and off-the-cuff ideas. I remember that during one holiday season, Tom Volz, our vice president of marketing, came up to me and said, "You know, Howard, instead of just sending the usual Christmas cards this year, let's do some-thing different for a change. Why don't we take advantage of the talent at Southwest?"

The talent Tom was referring to was Tony Brigmon and Mark and Julie Emmick. Tony was a reservations agent who eventually became our corporate goodwill ambassador. Mark worked in the mailroom at Southwest. He and his wife, Julie, sang profession-ally.

"What have you got in mind, Tom?" I asked him.

"Here's my idea. Let's do a little record, and call it 'Merry Christmas Southwest Style.' I've checked the prices. We can re-cord the songs, stamp the record, print the covers, and mail the records for around ninety cents each—about the same as mailing customized Christmas cards."

I was all for the idea—especially since I could be part of it. I had been singing solo in my church choir ever since high school. So on one side of the record I sang "White Christmas" in my tongue-in-cheek Bing Crosby imitation. The Emmicks sang a traditional Christmas duet on the same side. On the other side, Tony Brigmon sang an original song he wrote for the occasion called "Christmas Southwest Style." Everyone in the company loved receiving their special Christmas record. The local press—and even the *Wall Street Journal*—picked up the story.

Spontaneity pops up in unexpected places, often with surprising results. At Southwest, we often used films to supplement our training. Once we were making a training film for future flight attendants on how to handle an unruly passenger. This particular dramatization focused on a passenger who insisted on carrying a piece of luggage that did not fit anywhere on board the plane. The passenger had also refused to check the item—a large, gift-wrapped box.

Since we wanted to give trainees insight into how to handle such a situation, we used a Southwest attendant instead of a professional actress. For the part of the passenger we hired an actress and instructed her to be stubborn and disagreeable. We asked the attendant, whose name was Cindy, to respond as she actually would in a real-life situation.

When the actress boarded the airplane, she immediately went to her seat, holding the large gift-wrapped box in her lap. As she normally would do, Cindy came down the aisle to instruct the passenger that carry-on items had to be stowed before take-off.

"I'm sorry, ma'am," she said cheerfully. "You'll have to put that box in the overhead rack or under the seat in front of you."

"It won't fit," the woman retorted.

"Well, for safety reasons we'll have to find some place to put it. You cannot hold it during the flight. It cannot block the aisles or the emergency exists either, so you'll have to give it to me. I promise to find a safe place for it," Cindy said, reaching for the box.

The actress clutched the box tightly and said, "My son just gave me this as a birthday gift. It is an expensive set of glassware, and I don't want it broken. There is no way you're going to take it away from me! I'm gonna hold it on my lap!" The actress spoke with a forcefulness that sounded absolutely real.

At this point, Cindy also forgot this was a training film. She and the actress-passenger began tugging at their respective ends of the box until the multicolored gift wrap was flying about the cabin.

"You either give me this box or I'm going to shove it up your —!" Cindy screamed. That's when she remembered that she was on camera.

We all laughed. But at the same time we also realized that Cindy's outburst made a valuable point about how our emotions can get the best of us. We decided to leave this spontaneous dramatization in the training film. Employees from every department had a good laugh talking about the incident.

For the most part, we had more fun with our customers than this training video implied. During our flights, attendants sometimes announced that whoever had the largest hole in their right sock would win a bottle of champagne. We'd have a planeload of passengers remove their shoes and compare socks. A flight attendant might unravel a roll of toilet paper down the aisle from the front of the airplane to the back and ask passengers to guess the number of individual sheets between two points. The person who offered the closest answer would receive a prize.

At Southwest, we tried to redefine the work experience for our employees—and the product experience for our customers—to ensure that everyone enjoyed their association with the airline. Just about every one of our competitors felt that flying from Dallas to Austin meant just getting on the plane in one city and off the plane in another—but not us!

Another example of the spontaneous fun we had at Southwest came out of a friendly bet with Herb Kelleher, our board chair. When the airline started service between Dallas and Oklahoma City and Dallas and Tulsa, I made an offhanded remark: "Herb, I'll bet we can board more passengers from Oklahoma City than the people in Tulsa."

"You've got yourself a bet," Herb responded. "Let's come up with some stakes that will involve our people in a fun way."

Herb and I devised what we called the steak-and-beans contest. I took Oklahoma City and Herb took Tulsa. Whoever boarded the most passengers during the first sixty days of operation would win. Winning team members would fly from Oklahoma to Dallas, where they would enjoy a lavish steak dinner served by the losers. Then the losers would eat a simple dinner of beans.

As it turned out, Herb and his team from Tulsa won. The night of the dinner, Herb wore a gold crown and sat on a large throne. From his regal perch, Herb directed the losing team to serve food, pour water, and take away used forks and knives. We were at his beck and call until all the winners finished eating.

When the victors' meal was complete, we losers—I, in my striped prisoner's suit, and my fellow teammates—sat at cramped, unadorned tables to eat beans. What we lost in decorum we more than made up for in increased morale and team spirit.

Perhaps you don't see the benefit of making fun an integral part of your company. But ask yourself what you have to lose. Consider how developing this kind of spontaneity and good-natured comradery might benefit your company. Try to visualize the rapport that this can create between company and customer or between manager and staff. Imagine an uplifting spirit in your company that elevates productivity and encourages teamwork and harmony.

I urge you to encourage spontaneity. It is as natural in the human spirit as change and turbulence are in the business environment. I'm convinced that, during the coming years, the two will do much to complement each other.

Systematic Fun

Although much of our fun at Southwest was spontaneous, we also had formal, or systematic, ways of bringing diversion to the organization. Systematic diversion reduces pressure and helps sustain an organization's momentum. The four simple techniques we used at Southwest reduced boredom and boosted enthusiasm. Perhaps your company can benefit from adapting some of these ideas.

CREATE PROGRAMS, POLICIES, AND PROCEDURES
THAT GENERATE FUN

The fun spirit at Southwest made it an enjoyable place to work. Because we were happy, we projected positive energy in our dealings with customers. All these good feelings did not come about by accident: they were the result of a concerted effort by everybody in the company.

The notion of making Southwest a fun place to work was specifically cited in our statement of purpose. In practice, this spirit included everyone on the senior management team and every employee who wanted to be part of it. Every executive and employee may not have possessed the greatest sense of humor. But everyone tended to get swept up in the lighthearted spirit that permeated every aspect of our operation.

There was a strong element of fun in our advertising campaigns, our customer service policies, our employee incentive and recognition programs, our training and education—as well as our internal and external communications. Once you become aware of how important fun is to the success of your company, you can start building it into every aspect of what you do.

REDUCE JOB OR TASK REDUNDANCY

At Southwest, we strived to make every task as reasonable and uncomplicated as possible. We eliminated busywork wherever we identified it, removing unnecessary steps and complexities. We encouraged managers and supervisors to find ways to eliminate repetitiveness and redundancy in all areas—particularly their own responsibilities and tasks.

Wherever possible, we broke routine. Each Friday, we relaxed the dress code. Employees could wear jeans and shorts and other casual clothing. We called it Get-Down Friday. When appropriate, employees were also encouraged to dress in the spirit of the season. At Christmas, some flight attendants dressed as Santa and Mrs. Claus. They handed candy and token gifts to passengers. At Easter, bunnies answered our telephones, and at Halloween, witches and skeletons worked the ticket counters.

We relied on employees who routinely handled a particular task to offer suggestions on how that task could be made less redundant and more enjoyable. We urged our people to be self-sufficient, to resolve problems and answer questions on their own. This fostered a sense of responsibility and created more effective customer service.

At Southwest, we encouraged employees to examine their own habits and on-the-job practices. We asked them to look for ways to change what they did day to day in order to reduce redundancy, increase productivity, and make their jobs more enjoyable.

INVOLVE EMPLOYEES IN EXPERIENCES OUTSIDE
THEIR JOB DESCRIPTIONS

Whenever a company makes a new capital addition—whether a new plant, a significant new product line, or a new office building—it should be treated as an event. If possible, these events should be turned into celebrations.

The purchase of a new airplane was always a big event at Southwest—particularly during its early years. Each time the senior management team went to Seattle to pick up a new airplane, several employees were selected to make the trip with us. We also asked the flight crew to invite their spouses. The entire contingent took a scheduled flight to Seattle early in the day. The following morning, we flew the new plane home to Dallas.

Our stay in Seattle began with a tour of the city. Employees had a chance to visit and learn about a city they may never have otherwise seen. In order to learn more about the planes that carried their customers every day, employees were given a tour of the Boeing plant. The evening in Seattle ended at a banquet dinner with Boeing executives. Here employees had a chance to learn something about the business of building airplanes and the people who build them. The following morning, we boarded the new plane, toasted it, and flew it home.

When an employee was invited to make the "delivery flight," as it was called, it was considered a badge of honor. That one gesture gave our people an opportunity to have fun, a change of pace, a broadening experience, and a sign of recognition. Is there something similar that can be instituted at your company—perhaps a night on the town or a company-paid weekend? Once you start thinking creatively in this direction, the options are almost endless.

To involve our people in experiences outside their day-to-day tasks, we also held regular management conferences. They were designed so that people could come in on an early flight—and spend four or five hours learning and interacting with their colleagues. These conferences boosted enthusiasm and productivity. Middle managers were given sneak previews of new products or new marketing campaigns.

Then, at some point in the afternoon, luncheon was served.

After another hour or two of informal talks, everyone returned home. These day-long conferences proved to be a short, sweet, and potent way to keep our people excited, dedicated, and immersed in team spirit.

To keep employees in touch with parts of the company outside their daily experience, we sent them videotaped messages from various members of the senior management team. These videos were a good way to say hello and pass along important information and temporarily to transport employees out of their daily routines and into whatever scenarios we created—training, informational, or motivational. Naturally we injected a spirit of humor and fun into all of these videos, and they played an important part in companywide communication.

OFFER REGULAR AND FREQUENT RECOGNITION FOR A JOB WELL DONE

One of the most gratifying things a company can do for employees is to honor them in front of their peers with recognition for excellence. At Southwest, we gave awards throughout the year for various achievements.

When I arrived at the airline, the system for employee recognition was inadequate. Employees received a pin and a banquet for five years of service: that was about it.

To better recognize commitment and professionalism among our people, I created an annual awards ceremony and introduced several new awards. One was the Founder's Award, which went to the employee of the year. Each department submitted one candidate, and the senior officers picked the winner.

We looked for someone who was contributing far beyond what was expected—an employee who exuded the kind of enthusiasm, pride, and commitment we wanted all our people to have. The employee of the year was someone who contributed as much to fellow employees, customers, and the community as he or she did to the company.

We also gave the President's Award. This came from my office and went to an employee who did something outstanding in the area of safety or customer service. This award included cash, an engraved plaque, and photographs of the dedication ceremony.

The Good Neighbor Award went to an individual or organization outside the company who most supported the airline during the year. The award recognized the commitment of an individual to Southwest even though he or she was not employed by the airline.

The biggest tribute we made at Southwest was naming a plane in an individual's (or group's) honor. We named only four such planes in the three years I was there.

We named the first plane the *Herbert D. Kelleher*. Herb was our chairman, cofounder, and acting president after Muse left Southwest and before I joined the airline. Herb was also an attorney and had fought and won a number of legal battles that threatened to put Southwest out of business. We painted his name under the cockpit windows and threw a surprise ceremony.

Later, whenever there was a rough landing with the *Herbert D. Kelleher,* Herb would receive letters from passengers complaining that his plane had square wheels. This proved to be an excellent way to communicate one-on-one with customers through a personalized and witty response to the lighthearted complaint.

We named the second plane the *Rollin W. King,* after the company's other cofounder. That plane was dedicated in Seattle. We had teeshirts made for the ceremony that said, "I flew the *Rollin W. King.''* We distributed the teeshirts to passengers who flew the plane home from Seattle, in Rollin's honor.

We named the third plane the *Captain Donald Ogden.* Captain O, as we called him, was our vice president in charge of flight operations. The dedication was part of his retirement tribute. The fourth and final plane was dedicated at the company's tenth anniversary. We named it the *Winning Spirit* to honor the collective commitment and enthusiasm of every employee at Southwest.

When we did something at Southwest we always stretched its impact as far as we could. Whenever possible, we rolled the crescendo of one event or campaign into the seed of the next, never allowing the momentum to fade.

One of our most successful recognition and incentive programs was a three-month program called the Love Token Awards. One reason for its success was that it came directly from our customers.

The Love Token was a coin, about the size of a quarter. One

side read "Southwest Airlines"; the other side read "Love Token." We sent a package of tokens to our regular customers, all of whose names we kept on file.

We asked these customers to take the tokens with them whenever they flew Southwest. Any time a Southwest employee did something above and beyond the call of duty, a customer could say thank-you by giving the employee a Love Token. Employees collected the Love Tokens for ninety days, after which they could be redeemed for prizes. The employee with the most Love Tokens won a full-length fur coat or a major home appliance.

During my three years at Southwest, the company continued to develop ideas that added enjoyment to everyone's job. Some were spontaneous; others were created systematically. But if I had to pick one adjective to describe the experience at Southwest, it would be *fun.*

I believe that our commitment to having a good time while we worked was an important reason that quality and productivity remained high. There is no question in my mind that our commitment to a happy environment was one of the most important reasons that revenues and profits kept going up—to the point that the company tripled in size.

In many respects, we were lucky at Southwest. The economy in Texas was particularly strong at the time, and it could be argued that fun was easy for us. Maybe if times had been uncertain or difficult, the spirit of fun would not have been as easy to generate. Nevertheless, it would have been just as important— maybe even more so.

I can't say that it was easy to generate the same kind of joyful spirit when we took the reins at Braniff. Yet even in that airline's darkest days, we strived to maintain a sense of humor. This helped keep the situation in perspective and greatly reduced tension and friction.

You will recall my advice about having fun in the workplace: take your job seriously, but always keep a sense of humor about yourself. Taking one's job seriously should always be a priority, but taking oneself too seriously can be dangerous. When egos become inflated, the team loses its cohesiveness and energy. When the self becomes more highly regarded than the company, the organization suffers. Without team spirit and a sense of humor, productivity and harmony are compromised. Eventually, this is reflected in product quality and profitability.

In today's business climate, uncertainty is a given for any company. Fortunes can change literally overnight—and this will affect everyone who works for that organization. Still, the leaders of a company can offer their people one constant in both good times and bad—a work experience that is enjoyable and fun. You owe it to them, to your customers—and to yourself.

8

Follow the Yellow Brick Rule:
Seven Golden Roads to Corporate Virtue

One of the keys to averting and coping with crisis is honesty. Dedication to truth and an ethical standard ensures respect for employees, customers, the environment—everybody and everything touched by the company. In the cutthroat atmosphere that pervaded the 1980s, such thinking may have been viewed as naive. But in the 1990s, a growing number of business leaders have come to recognize that few things have a more beneficial effect on a company's bottom line than a stable and irreproachable system of values and integrity.

I learned the importance of honesty long before I had an opportunity to lead a major company. Fortunately, I was blessed with parents who were committed to the virtue of the golden rule. They simply would not tolerate anything less than completely honest and ethical behavior on the part of their children.

I learned a significant lesson about integrity at the age of nine. At the time, one of my best buddies was a boy named Dean Spencer. Dean was a tall, scraggly, redheaded kid who lived on the farm down the road from ours. He was a year older than I, and the lesson I learned through my association with him has stayed with me all these years.

One day, as Dean and I were walking into town to buy comic books, he made an intriguing proposition: Why should we spend twenty cents for two comic books when we could just as easily spend ten cents? All we had to do was slip the second comic book inside the first—and pay for one.

Our first attempt to steal a comic book proved to be a phenomenal success. We walked into Blake's Music and Book Store ready to implement the plan Dean had so carefully outlined. We roamed through the aisles, acting a little bored to avoid drawing any undue attention. We were, of course, careful not to appear so bored that we looked suspicious.

As we strolled through the store, our faces, gestures, and occasional remarks were designed to make us appear as low-profile and inconspicuous as possible. We made our way to the comic book section, and then we thumbed through the stack nonchalantly, trying to show only casual interest. We narrowed our choices down to a couple favorites; made a quick but inconspicuous search of our surroundings, slipped one comic book into the center of the other, and made for the counter.

Sweat emerging from every pore, we went to the register, offered our most innocent faces, and placed a dime on the counter. The cashier accepted our ten cents, as well as our sinless expressions, and we knew we had accomplished our mission: we had stolen a comic book. As we turned toward the door, I restrained a fierce impulse to run. Dean and I smiled coyly at each other as we strutted proudly to the street.

During the course of the next few weeks, Dean and I filched a few more comic books. With each experience, we were becoming more proficient. Our nonchalant attitude and our sleight-of-hand were approaching perfection. We were successful thieves—and proud of it.

One day, I decided it was time for a bigger challenge. As it happened, I needed new reflectors for my bicycle. Since I had no money for the reflectors, I was left with two options—either go without or steal them. Based on my success with the comic books, I chose thievery.

One Thursday after school, I walked into the local Western Auto Store and spotted a rack full of shiny red bicycle reflectors on the other side of the store.

As usual, I conducted an obligatory sweep of the store to make sure that my criminal activity would go unnoticed by the cashier or busybody patrons. When I was certain that nobody was watching, I quickly reached over the counter, grabbed two of the brightest red reflectors I had ever seen, and slipped them into my hip pocket. Then, as I headed for the door, a voice of unknown origin sent a shiver up my spine: "Young man, what have you got in your pocket?" the authoritative, resonant voice asked. The voice belonged to the store manager; but, to me, it could have been the voice of my conscience or the voice of the Creator.

"Nothing," I answered meekly. My mind raced. On one hand, I hoped that the manager would accept my answer and let me leave. But somewhere deep down I secretly wished that my conscience would give way and force me to confess right there and then. But before I could resolve my conflict, the voice spoke again: "I saw you put some reflectors in your pocket, young man," the voice said. "And I want you to give them to me right now."

As I turned around, I saw that the voice had the body of a large man connected to it. That body was now positioned between me and the door. Frightened more than I had ever been in my nine years, I took the reflectors out of my pocket and placed them in the store manager's hand.

"I want you to go home and tell your parents what you have done here today," the man said. "Then I want you back in this store tomorrow, with one of your parents, to give me an apology." My illicit treasure returned to its rightful place behind the counter, I dropped my head and walked out of the store.

On my way home I thought about what I had done. I knew it was wrong. It seemed to me that taking the reflectors was a far worse crime than slipping one comic book inside another. The comic book scheme was a prank, but taking the reflectors was stealing. If I had been older, and if it had been a car I tried to steal, I might well be heading to jail instead of for home.

The minute I walked into the house, I immediately confessed to my parents what I had done. My mother cried harder than I had ever seen her cry before. That was the part that hurt me the most—to watch my mother crying her eyes out because of my dishonesty.

The next day Dad firmly escorted me to the Western Auto Store. We walked in and located the manager. Feeling ashamed and foolish, I looked him in the eye, said I was sorry, and promised that I would never do anything like that again. I've kept my word.

This early incident, though frightening and upsetting, played a major role in setting the course for ethics in my life. It forever etched on my mind the value of honesty. At age nine, it struck me that, if it never did anything else, honesty would at least save me from being reprimanded. As I grew up, I came to realize that living honestly and ethically wasn't only a matter of avoiding punishment: it was a code by which civilized human beings ran their lives and their businesses.

Golden Rule Companies

As far as I'm concerned, there isn't a whole lot of difference between individuals who conduct themselves honestly and ethically and corporations that do the same. Since my youthful bout with dishonesty, I've tried my best to live by the golden rule. When I am assessing an individual or a company, I try to determine whether these values are evident. A golden rule company lives by a standard of operation drawn from a biblical proverb meant to guide individuals in all phases of their lives: "Do unto others as you would have them do unto you."

We have heard this proverb many times, but too many business leaders have forgotten its meaning. The attitudes and actions of certain executives, from Wall Street to Hollywood, indicate a greed and self-centeredness that ignores the needs, wants, and basic rights of others. Most often, as with Wall Street's Drexel Burnham Lambert junk bond scandal, the money fever, the preoccupation with short-term gains, and the bias toward vice over virtue eventually prove fatal. Unfortunately, when self-centeredness swallows a company, it also consumes many innocent families and hard-earned fortunes in the process.

In order to force companies to think before proceeding with a takeover, a New Jersey court recently ruled that employees who lost their jobs due to a hostile buyer can sue the predatory corporation. I agree with the spirit of this ruling but also feel that it sets a dangerous legal precedent.

Responsible corporations and business leaders have an obligation to police themselves. Self-policing begins when the leaders of a company lay down a code of conduct and ethics that comes from the top and is enforced at all levels. These codes must guide the actions of every employee, every day, in every situation. Stiff penalties must be administered when the codes are breached.

Ethics is a discipline that must be practiced at all times. Selective ethics is an oxymoron. For a golden rule company, honest and ethical behavior are a way of life.

I recently had the pleasure of working with what I consider an outstanding example of a golden rule company. The company was Alco Standard Corporation—a $4 billion concern headquartered in Philadelphia that employs 16,000 people.

The following are portions of a statement from Alco Standard's 1990 Corporate Strategy Guideline. It was signed by Alco's chair and CEO, Ray Mundt.

> I want Alco to continue to be a company of integrity, built upon enduring values and committed to honesty when dealing with all of our constituents. I want Alco to be respected within the business community and an involved participant in community affairs.
>
> We are a disciplined company, serious about our responsibilities to both shareholders and employees—a company that demonstrates its commitment to employees through its support of training and skill development programs. Alco must be a company with solid, well-trained and highly motivated management, committed to the achievement of our goals. Our employees also have important personal goals and objectives, and I want Alco to be a place that helps individuals become what they want to be.
>
> Alco must always be in a strong financial condition—always in control, no surprises. We will run the company in such a way as to be viewed by shareholders as well-managed, committed to shareholder value—a company that knows where it is going and how it is going to get there. Alco is a company that respects its employees and managers—one

that consistently rewards its shareholders and maintains credibility within the financial community.

Corporations, like individuals, have distinct personalities and characters. A company's employees, shareholders, suppliers, and customers—and the general public—develop an opinion based on the way that company looks, talks, and acts. That opinion has a pervasive effect on the interest and productivity of all constituents—and their interaction with the company.

A truly empowering relationship between a company and its constituents can come about only when all parties understand that ethics underlie all actions, policies, and decisions. Because of the fast pace at which we do business today, such values tend to get lost in the shuffle. Sometimes they slip out of the hands of those at the helm, but more often than not they simply are relegated to low-priority status. This oversight can prove highly destructive and even fatal.

Over the years, I have watched and listened. I have hypothesized, experimented, and learned from my mistakes. I now believe that there are certain dimensions of ethical behavior that are critical to the long-term success of all businesses. What follows are seven precepts that are absolutely necessary to the well-being of a company and all its constituents.

The Seven Corporate Graces

HONESTY

A golden rule company speaks and seeks the truth. It lets constituents know, through direct and open communication, where they stand. It requests the same in return. Among other things, honesty includes frank and forthright communication with the media.

In 1988, the government of the United States (according to published reports) knew of a commercial plane returning from Europe that might become the object of a terrorist bombing. Nevertheless, the government and the airline chose not to alert the public. Soon after the government became aware of the threat, a Pan American jet exploded in midair over Scotland. Everybody on board died. In the wake of this incident, certain governmental departments were severely chastised—and rightfully so.

About a year later, someone threatened a Delta Airlines flight from Miami to the United Kingdom. Delta chose to warn the public—at the risk of losing a considerable number of customers. As it turned out, the threat turned out to be a hoax, and the perpetrator was apprehended. A short time later, customers began returning to Delta, and the airline picked up a substantial number of new customers.

As a result of the airline's frankness in the face of crisis, people felt that Delta would alert them to any possibility of danger. Corporate honesty resulted in customer loyalty. A lot of people were surprised by this turn of events, but I was not one of them.

Some media commentators have argued that honesty broke Braniff's back. I disagree. The debate centered around an incident involving myself and a Dallas reporter.

During a difficult moment at Braniff, a journalist with the *Dallas Morning News* asked me a simple question that was one of the hardest I ever have had to answer: "Can you guarantee that Braniff will still be in operation one year from now?"

My honest answer was a terse no. I am not a soothsayer: I cannot make predictions in an unpredictable world. I certainly was in no position to offer assurances about the future of a corporation that was in the midst of considerable turbulence.

If the reporter had used a word other than *guarantee,* I might have been able to say something encouraging. I proceeded to ask him if he could guarantee that his paper would be around in a year? Unlike Braniff, the *Dallas Morning News* was experiencing an upturn in its fortunes. Nevertheless, the reporter said he was not about to offer any such assurance. In any case, he was interested in my answer—not my question.

The following day, the headline in the *Dallas Morning News* read, "Braniff Chief Uncertain If Airline Will Survive." Technically, the headline was true, but it was not an accurate reflection of what I had said.

After telling the reporter that I could not guarantee Braniff's survival, I proceeded to explain how optimistic I was about the airline's future and how all Braniff's constituents were committed to its endurance. But somehow all of that got lost in my headline-grabbing initial reply.

I do not think my honesty in that situation changed the outcome for Braniff—although some argue otherwise. Nevertheless, the point is moot from an ethical perspective.

As part of the ethics curriculum at Harvard University, Professor Kenneth Goodpastor wrote and taught a case study based on the Braniff bankruptcy. It was called "Ethics of Bankruptcy." Although Professor Goodpastor is no longer at Harvard, the case study is still offered there and at several other universities around the country.

The first time Professor Goodpastor taught the Braniff case was in 1984. My wife, Krista, and I, as well as Phil Guthrie, his wife, Beverly, and Dr. Don Beck, the noted industrial psychologist, sat in the classroom during the lesson. After Professor Goodpastor told of the circumstances leading up to the newspaper headline, he requested a show of hands in response to the following question: "How many of you think that Mr. Putnam should have lied to the reporter?"

I was distressed to see most of the students raise their hands—that the vast majority of young men and women in an ethics class at Harvard felt that I should have been less than candid.

As I reflect on the values that prevailed during the early and mid-1980s, perhaps I should not have been surprised that students responded in that way. Then again, I believe that this disregard for the truth had a lot to do with the precarious situation certain sectors of American business—particularly banking, real estate, and investment—found themselves as the new decade opened.

The question concerning whether I should have lied to the reporter is still asked by Harvard professors who teach the course in business ethics. I am happy to note that each year a larger percentage of students responds that I was right to tell the truth. To me, this indicates a positive shift in the attitudes of the men and women who will lead our businesses—and our country—as we enter the twenty-first century.

In the long term, honesty always proves worthwhile. Just as

Delta was able to attract new customers because it took a forthright stance in a tough situation, you and your business can also profit by this kind of forthrightness.

But what of Braniff? Although the airline eventually was put into Chapter 11, it survived as long as it did and had the strength to fly again because of the energy and urgency created by leaders who were willing to tell the truth. When the people within a company are dealt with evenhandedly, they are able to understand where they are and what needs to be accomplished before the situation can be improved. That is the only way to generate the kind of energy needed to avert and conquer crises.

INTEGRITY

A golden rule company remains faithful to its word.

Mother Teresa once said she never promised God that she would fulfill her commitments. She promised only that she would always be faithful to her commitments. Herein lies the essence of integrity.

A company must be faithful to its promises and its constituents. Generally, when an organization is dedicated to its commitments, the results take care of themselves.

The United States during the 1980s became a quick-fix, easy-out, instant-gratification society. The strength of our commitments was diluted by our tendency to stick to our word when it was convenient—and discard it when it became burdensome. When a bigger deal crossed our desk, or someone prettier or more handsome walked through the door, we changed our minds and our promises like we changed our clothes. We lost the riches of possibilities that sticking to our commitments may have afforded.

In a world that moves as fast as ours, opportunities present themselves at ever-increasing speeds and frequencies. The desire to capitalize on every opportunity has undermined our ability to make firm commitments and see them through. As businesses and individuals, we often act like tennis players—bouncing from foot to foot, waiting to chase the ball depending on how it comes over the net. This approach may work in tennis—but in business it results in chaos.

American society has a reputation for being obsessed with instant gratification. One aspect of this is an unhealthy affinity for things that can be thrown away. Our infatuation with disposability has eroded our integrity to the point that our word is often seen as just one more throw-away commodity. We all have dealt with companies whose products don't live up to their advertisements—as well as people who give their word and don't feel obliged to honor it if another course of action becomes more advantageous.

When I began speaking professionally, one of my first scheduled engagements was in the dead of winter at a university in the Northeast. The school was two hours from the LaGuardia Airport in New York City, and the weather was likely to be slushy and cold. Moreover, the university was able to offer only a modest fee.

All things considered, this did not promise to be the most desirable engagement. Still, I felt the opportunity was important. The university had launched a lecture series on ethics, and I thought that the program deserved my time and attention.

A few days before I was to fly to New York, a large organization invited me to St. Thomas to speak for an hour and then bask in the sun. For that pleasure, they would pay me considerably more than my normal fee, as well as cover all my expenses. There was only one catch: the St. Thomas lecture fell on the same day as the lecture at the university. It was impossible to do both.

I thought of calling my future hosts in the Northeast and telling them that something important had come up. The trip there would not be very profitable or convenient or fun—nor did it offer me much potential for future business. Nevertheless, I went: I had given my word, and that is the only currency over whose value I have complete control.

As businesspeople, we must be committed to what we say. When we maintain our integrity through simple promises to each other, that integrity finds its way into all our dealings. It has a direct effect on the profits we earn for shareholders and the products and services we offer our customers.

Try to imagine doing business in a climate where promises are kept simply because they have been made. Roger Smith of General Motors has taken some heat because he stated that a town's jobs were safe—only to close the plant the following day, putting thousands of people out of work. An Academy Award–winning film called *Roger and Me* documented the story of what happened to the laid-off workers and their families.

For the most part, however, we tend to overlook such behavior because, after all, business is business. As far as I'm concerned, this is one of the biggest failings and cop-outs of the business world. Too many people in corporate America have been operating under the misconception that business is a world separate from other worlds—that the ethical standards one applies to business are different from those applied to other areas of life.

You've probably heard the old expression, "All's fair in love and war." Some people expand on that to read, "All's fair in love, war, and business."

Think about how our lives would be affected if that kind of thinking applied to community, education, family, religion, and art. Now think about this: If leaders of large corporations don't stand by their word, they are threatening the sanctity of all these other institutions.

The idea that anything goes in business is used to justify murder by organized crime, as when a hit man says, "This guy was a friend of mine, but I had to kill him because of business."

There is not a far jump from this reasoning to what Roger Smith did in the name of business. I have no doubt that Roger is a good family man who has taught his children to live by the golden rule. But I'm sorry, Roger—you can't have it both ways. Integrity and hypocrisy just don't mix. One way or the other, we are going to have to conduct ourselves by a single set of values.

COURAGE

A golden rule company operates innovatively, beyond existing frameworks and systems. It has the patience to think and act on a broad scale and for the long term, and to forgo instant gratification. It has the spirit to face hardship with the same value system that it uses to face success.

Courage is a multifaceted value—both in business and in life. Courage has many faces, some of which are particularly important to a senior executive.

A business leader needs to look beyond his or her own needs.

First, he or she must make personal needs secondary to those of the company. Then, he or she must have the courage to look beyond the company's needs and consider the needs of all those affected by the company, including stockholders, customers, suppliers, and creditors.

A courageous business leader looks beyond the needs of a company's stakeholders to the needs of society at large. Depending on the business, such vision proceeds further outward to encompass the entire world. Such is the courage of broad-scale thought. As we move toward global integration of business and society, such thinking becomes increasingly important.

Another face of courage involves long-term thought—that is, the ability to take actions and make decisions that transcend their immediate impact. Business leaders with this kind of vision are concerned about creating something that endures and has value for future generations.

Before finalizing a major decision, certain American Indian tribes would consider its effect on seven successive generations. Some Japanese corporations calculate the impact of their decisions 250 years into the future. Although most American companies don't concern themselves with such long-term thinking, perhaps they should seriously consider it. Our years on this planet are limited, and we ought to be concerned about the legacy we leave our children—and the generations who succeed them.

A third face of courage is innovation. At one time, American business had a virtual monopoly on new thought and new technology. Since the end of World War II, however, we have allowed that to become the domain of Japanese and German companies. Nevertheless, there are signs that innovation is returning to some American industries. We continue to be aggressive in research and development in aircraft manufacturing and related technologies, fiberoptics, supercomputers, and biomedical technology such as magnetic resonance imaging and genetics engineering.

The Boeing Company is on the leading edge in producing sophisticated, high-quality aircraft and navigational and operational systems. One way Boeing stays on top is by sharing technology with competitors. Although some observers have criticized Boeing for taking this approach, the company has ensured its success by not ignoring excellence elsewhere in the world.

Rather than engaging in costly battles with innovators in the same business, Boeing takes advantage of that excellence by forming alliances and partnerships with companies that might otherwise be competitors. Instead of losing market share to an adversary, Boeing increases it through creative control over its processes and techniques so that its generosity is not abused.

Today I see courage in the leadership at companies such as Alco Standard and its leaders Ray Mundt, CEO, and Dick Gozon, COO. These two men set strict ethical standards and stick by them. They allow the companies they acquire to remain independent. They do not bureaucratize and overmanage. They refuse to fall prey to the pressures and weaknesses created through leveraged buyouts by working with a formula of internally generated funds. Senior management at Alco thinks, talks, and acts long term. All employees—not just a select few—share in the profitability of the organization.

Donald Peterson, former chair at Ford Motor Company, also had courage. He had the grit to pursue excellence and invest in the future of the American car industry. He and his people at Ford undertook the massive $6 billion Taurus project while competitors whined and groused about foreign competition. The Taurus project could have taken Ford under had it been thinking and acting in the short term, but Peterson's vision was focused far down the road.

In the short term, he had to take the heat from analysts and investors who screamed that profitability did not meet expectations. But Peterson had the courage and foresight to stick to his long-term plans. By 1990, Peterson's innovative, far-reaching planning came to fruition. Ford's competitiveness in the domestic and foreign market is laudable, and the Taurus is considered one of the best—if not the best—car in its class.

Courage allows us, as individuals and as corporate entities, to dedicate ourselves to a purpose. Courage allows us, as leaders, to maintain commitment to our constituents against the lure of short-term gains and the easy way out.

FAIRNESS

A golden rule company is fair and sincere in all its negotiations—particularly employee negotiations. It resolves all disputes objectively with an emphasis on the facts. It competes and prices in a forthright and unhostile manner.

There is no universal rule or definition of fairness. Within the limits of the law, it is a value determined by the parties involved in a relationship. From a practical standpoint, fairness begins with communication—by talking candidly about the needs and wants of both parties.

In a corporation, fairness starts with the CEO. He or she is in the unique position of having a direct relationship with representatives from all constituent groups—members of the board, shareholders and investors, senior executives, managers, labor leaders, employee groups, and even customers. The CEO should be the role model for equitable relations among all members of a company.

Trust grows from relationships where neither party uses knowledge, influence, resources, authority, or any other means to gain more than what is equitable—even when such opportunities present themselves. This means not that companies or individuals should discard advantages they may have in relationships or negotiations, but that such advantages should not be abused.

Fairness can generate loyalty. Delta Airlines has for many years faithfully followed a policy of not laying off employees during lean times. As an alternative, the airline has offered pension incentives or carried employees on the payroll until a more productive solution was found. A few years ago, in an expression of gratitude for this generous policy, the employees all contributed to buy another aircraft for Delta's fleet. I was moved when I heard that.

Delta rewarded employee commitment and service by searching for an alternative to layoffs. This created employee loyalty and appreciation almost unmatched in American big business. Imagine your employees pulling together to buy your company a new plant, a new supercomputer, or a new facility simply as a thank-you. What would that say about how well the company was managed—and the role of fairness in generating loyalty?

Fairness must also extend to competitors. We no longer operate in a world where it is productive to try to put your competitor out of business. Too much time and energy are required to contend with the ever-changing needs of employees and customers to waste valuable resources on bitter rivalries.

After Lamar Muse left Southwest, he and his son Mike formed their own airline. They called it Muse Air and positioned it to directly compete against Southwest. Lamar publicly announced his strategy: his airline would be the David that would take on and defeat the Southwest Goliath. Around Dallas, people jokingly called Muse's company Revenge Air.

Instead of escalating a spiteful and potentially destructive competition, we ran advertisements that welcomed Muse Air to the "Friendly Skies of Dallas and Love Field." We ran those ads because their message reflected the spirit of our company. At Southwest, we competed internally, matching and surpassing our own standards and goals. We fought to provide our customers with a better product. This left little time and energy to fight against our competitors.

This advertising campaign so disarmed the combativeness of Muse Air that the employees of that company signed a petition of gratitude and sent it to me, thanking Southwest for its warm and friendly competitive spirit.

One long-standing antagonist to fairness is the double standard. Double standards still exist in business. You can find them in the salary gap between equally competent male and female executives, the level of opportunity offered nonminority versus minority employees, and the preferential treatment certain "friendly" suppliers and vendors receive, even in a so-called open bid for services.

Although the double standard has diminished somewhat over the past twenty or thirty years, it is still a prevalent problem that undercuts every man and woman's right to an equal opportunity, both in and out of the workplace.

BENEVOLENCE TO THE ENVIRONMENT

A golden rule company treats the environment with kindness, charity, and respect.

In the past, large corporations avoided complying with the recommendations of the Environmental Protection Agency and other government agencies that set standards to protect the environment. Compliance with environmental standards almost always increases costs. But in an age where the quality of the air we breathe and the water we drink threatens to poison us and our children, businesses must reconcile economic growth with the needs of the environment.

Because the airline industry was strictly regulated for so many years, it has a synergistic relationship with the Federal Aviation Agency. This long-standing partnership, although not without friction, has always worked to maximize the safety of the consumer and, to a somewhat lesser degree, the safety of the environment.

Over the past few decades, the private and public sectors have worked together to create high-bypass jet engines. Because these engines are smoke-free, they deposit no unburned jet-fuel residue into the environment. In some cases engine noise is reduced up to 50 percent.

In the long run, much of the technology developed to protect the environment has led to greater fuel efficiency, reduced energy costs, and lower fares for airline customers. Protecting the environment does not have to mean sacrificing customer service.

Our environment is nearing its maximum tolerance level. Weather patterns are erratic, the ozone is weakening, rain forests are disappearing, and acid rain still pelts the earth. The increased attention the environment is receiving from the scientific community, environmental organizations, and independent citizens throughout the world is evidence that nature can no longer be left to fend for itself.

As executives, we are learning that corporate responsibility extends far beyond the bottom line. It includes responsibility for the environment that gives us all life. Ultimately, to protect the interests of our stakeholders, we must protect the environment. If it is destroyed, not much else will matter.

We are stewards on this planet, not landlords. That means we have an obligation to preserve the earth's natural state and no right to tamper with its well-being. If, as corporations, we expect to continue operating in this environment, we must safeguard it.

Changing what we make and how we make it often takes time. As leaders we must dedicate ourselves and our companies to that change. We must begin the transformation immediately. In the meantime, though, we also can change how we administer our business.

I recently was made aware of a small company in California that is doing its part. For a newsletter it sends to 400,000 people this company used to use virgin paper—that is, paper made from newly cut trees. In 1989 the company started using recycled paper. This single move saves over 200 trees a year, almost 85,000 gallons of water, and more than 50,000 kilowatt hours of electricity. It reduces solid-waste pollution by 36 cubic yards and air pollution by nearly 400 pounds.

Every company can take similar action and use recycled paper, even just for its interoffice communications or its payroll checks. Has your company reduced its use of paper? Has it turned to electronic filing and data-transfer systems instead of generating paper triplicates of everything? Does it use recycled paper for its mailing envelopes? Does it recycle the paper it generates every day?

Most companies do not understand fully how their activities affect the environment. To be environmentally responsible, all companies need to take a hard look at all activities in which they are engaged. This includes the use of paper and other products necessary to maintain the organization, the production methods used to generate products, and the process by which wastes are disposed.

Through this kind of self-examination a company can create awareness about the impact of its activities on the environment and provide the motivation to create policies and products that are environmentally friendly.

There was a time when our business decisions affected only a small community of people—sometimes just the inhabitants of one small town. This is no longer the case. Virtually every company in America—regardless of size—now has to consider its impact on the global environment.

Over the next ten years there will be a mushrooming of environmental awareness. It has already begun to take hold at the grassroots level, spurred on by activists and special-interest groups. Many communities now have mandatory recycling of glass and paper products—and heavy penalties for individuals and companies who violate these guidelines.

More and more consumers ally themselves with companies

that respect the environment and foster its environmental well-being. I believe that in the very near future customer loyalty will be based on factors wholly unrelated to a company's service or product. Companies that are environmentally active will earn the respect and support of an ever-increasing number of consumers.

RECIPROCITY

A golden rule company contributes to the well-being of those who contribute to its well-being.

A company has many reciprocal relationships—including those with its employees, shareholders, and customers. Less obvious—but at least as important—are the relationships a company maintains between itself and the community within which it functions.

Reciprocity is a chameleon value. It takes the form of need satisfaction with employees, profitability with shareholders, quality of service with customers, and mutual obligation with the community.

Most companies are competent in terms of contributing to the well-being of shareholders. In this and other chapters, I have detailed the relationships between company and employee and between company and environment. But there is a reciprocal relationship between company and community and company and customer, as well.

Communities are the silent partners of corporations. A community provides the land on which a company operates, the road system, sanitation and other infrastructures, tax incentives, a labor pool, cultural diversions, and other amenities. In return, companies provide tax revenue and employment opportunities—and are a source for charitable and cultural donations.

Too many companies fail to recognize that a community can provide a home—not merely an address. When a company looks at the community as its home, a fuller and more beneficial relationship can develop. Think of the difference between how you treat a place you consider your home versus how you treat a place you perceive merely as the building where you are housed.

You would probably be willing to give a mere shelter nothing more than the mandatory attention necessary to prevent its deterioration for the period you were residing there. A home, on the other hand, you would approach with a desire to make an even more pleasing place.

We live in Plano, Texas—a community filled with the spirit of volunteerism and participation. In fact, the town has more citizen volunteers to serve on boards and commissions than it has positions to offer. In a recent call for volunteers, 1,500 candidates submitted applications for a capital-improvement committee.

Among the volunteers were people from companies like Frito-Lay, J. C. Penney, Electronic Data Systems, and Murata. These companies treat Plano like a home—to the benefit of both business and the community.

Let me give you one example of corporate volunteerism and its benefits. Since its inception in 1985, I have chaired an advisory board for a new civic center in Plano. One of the citizen members on the board was a vice president of Frito-Lay. Through the efforts of this one volunteer, we gained the expertise of the entire engineering staff of that company. Their engineers critiqued and advised our board on the civic center's plans. This kind of advice normally would have cost the residents of Plano thousands of dollars were it not donated by a community-minded business leader.

Electronic Data Systems also contributed to the Plano civic center. They helped secure and purchase the land on which the facility was built. With this kind of spirited volunteerism from corporate leaders, the Plano Center was completed on schedule—and at a cost of $700,000 under the $19.5 million estimate.

Employees of these companies and their families now have a first-rate civic center to enjoy. Because of the efforts of individual business leaders on behalf of their corporations, they and their companies have become respected contributors to our community.

In addition to the pride that is instilled by making meaningful contributions, both company and community have developed a relationship that is a model of the cooperation that is possible between the private and public sectors. This kind of favorable publicity improves a corporation's public image and attracts new businesses to a community.

Reciprocity also plays an important role in the relationship between a company and its customers. Initially, a company offers a product, and a customer offers money in exchange for it—but this is only the first level of reciprocity. Once the purchase is made, a company offers support for that product. Support may come in the form of technical assistance for new computer software, the availability of parts for automobiles, or guarantees should an item prove defective or unsuitable.

Companies that are concerned with building reciprocity with their customers are focused on forging long-term relationships rather than on making quick sales. Companies that plan to stay in business realize that they will be offering other products that may interest existing customers. If a customer is pleased with the support offered on already-purchased products, he or she is far more likely to want to continue doing business with that company.

I find that many companies do not fully recognize how important reciprocity is in their relationships with customers. When a consumer makes a purchase, along with the product or service paid for, he or she is also receiving a symbol of the company's mission, strategy, and culture. The quality of that product or service is nothing less than a statement of the company's regard for shareholders, employees, customers, and the general public— as well as an avowal of the company's commitment to excellence and benevolence to the environment.

When I think of a company that understands the importance of impeccable service, I think of a small West Coast retailer who prefers to remain anonymous.

One day, a manager at this particular establishment was showing a new employee the ropes. They were standing at the customer-service counter. Suddenly, a customer walked in and demanded her money back for a set of tires.

"I'm not happy with these tires, and I'd like to return them," she said to the customer-service clerk who happened to be on duty.

"Do you have your receipt, madam?" the clerk asked.

"Well, no. I'm sorry, I don't," the woman replied.

"Do you remember when you bought the tires?"

"Oh, it must have been almost a year ago."

"I see. And you bought the tires at this store?"

"Yes, I'm sure I did. Why, do you have another store nearby?"

"No, we don't."

"Then I am positive that I purchased them here."

"Very well, then," the clerk replied. "If you can remember how much the tires cost, I'd be glad to refund your money."

The trainee was a bit surprised that after a year, without a receipt and with the tires obviously worn, the store would return the customer's money. The trainee expressed his concern to the manager.

"Oh, that's not the half of it," the manager replied. "We stopped selling tires eighteen months ago."

The trainee's mouth started to open. But before he could utter a word, the manager explained: "At this store, the customer is always right. And when we say *always,* we mean *always!*"

JUSTICE

A golden rule company acts swiftly, conscientiously, and impartially if any corporate value—including the administration of justice—is violated.

Justice substantiates and protects all other corporate values. It is the unifying value—the watchdog value—that synthesizes honesty, integrity, courage, fairness, benevolence, and reciprocity into a cohesive and comprehensive system. Should any of the previous six values fail, justice must move in to close the gap.

Justice demands active participation in appropriate conduct, within both corporate and legal dictates. It also demands swift action if conduct exceeds the limits set by a company or legal system.

As a businessman—and a person—my decisions are driven by what I feel is right, within the limits of the law. Again, I thank my parents for teaching me to distinguish between right and wrong. As I have matured as a person and as a leader, justice—which I define as the administration of what is morally or legally right—has influenced my values more than any other concept. It is an integrating and culminating principle.

When a company fails to distinguish between right and wrong,

the fault usually lies with leaders who are weak in their administration of justice. Some of these leaders are unjust individuals.
Others have passive sets of values, the kind where honesty and
integrity are talked about but not practiced.

At Southwest, the question of justice often came into play—in
both large and small ways.

Early in the airline's history, as the carrier sought to turn to the
public, a lawsuit from a few frightened and envious competitors
forced Southwest into litigation. With persistence—and a willingness to work through the courts, Southwest was able to defeat
larger competitors who were unjustly looking to knock it out of
the race. It took three years, but justice was finally served, and
Southwest continued to grow.

Later in Southwest's history, when I came on board to oversee
its transition into a much larger airline, a number of employees
felt uncomfortable with the expansion. I had formed the new
senior management team, and we implemented techniques and
disciplines foreign to what Southwest employees had previously
experienced. This made many of the long-standing employees
unhappy. They thought the changes at Southwest were unnecessary and unjust—that the airline's history and tradition were
being discarded and its future strangled.

Although there was considerable concern during this period, I
tried to treat all employees equally—always doing my best to
maintain the values I have discussed in this chapter. In time, I
changed the minds of the vast majority of employees who op-
posed the changes we envisioned. Eventually, most of them became proponents of progress, and Southwest continued as the
strong team it had always been.

ACTIVE AND PASSIVE ETHICS

This chapter opened with my first lesson in ethics. As in many
lessons, right and wrong were pointed out to me after the fact.
As I indicated earlier, my greatest anxiety over the incident also
came after the fact. It was grounded more in the fear of being
reprimanded than in the conflict of right versus wrong.

Nine years after I got caught stealing reflectors for my bicycle,
I faced my first ethical dilemma in a business context. I knew then

what should be done. The anxiety was over whether I would act on it or not.

Just after midnight on August 1, 1955, twenty-one days before my eighteenth birthday, I began my first night's work at Chicago's Midway Airport. A man whom I'll call Tony Harper was assigned as my supervisor. We were in the forward belly of a Douglas DC-4 propeller-driven airplane and were about to unload the luggage. The conveyor belt had just been moved into place.

"Okay, kid," Tony said to me. "You start putting the bags on the conveyor. I've got work to do."

His was the manner of somebody young with a little bit of authority speaking to somebody younger who had absolutely no authority. Tony took a small hammer and a flashlight out of his pocket and started to bang open the latches on random pieces of luggage.

I noticed that Tony was carrying a small bag. When he found something he liked, he tossed it into his bag. I watched as he continued doing this all night long.

I was just a kid in the big city, and it was my first night on the job. I knew what was happening was wrong, but I was too frightened to act. I agonized over the situation but couldn't bring myself to do anything except continue to unload luggage. By morning, Tony had collected two grocery bags filled with items stolen from suitcases. I hadn't stopped him, and I was ashamed.

When I went home that morning, I couldn't sleep. I lay awake most of the day thinking about what I hadn't done. I was also worried about having to work with Tony again. I made up my mind that I would confront him if I saw him breaking into more luggage.

At midnight, when I arrived for work at Capital Airlines, I was once again assigned to work with Tony. This time we were in the bins, on the upper level of the airplane behind the cockpit. We weren't unloading luggage. On this night, we were unloading landing-gear tires. To my great relief, there was nothing for Tony to steal.

In order to unload the giant tires we had to place them on their sides on a long, steep conveyor belt. From there, the tires rode gently to the ground, where they were unloaded.

The fellow at the bottom of the belt wasn't paying attention as Tony tipped and rolled a tire onto the belt. But instead of resting it on its side, Tony carelessly let it roll down the belt. I watched in horror as 125 pounds of rubber rolled toward the ground.

A tire that size, moving at that speed, could have killed the man at the bottom of the conveyor belt. He noticed the tire just in time, however, and jumped out of the way. Fortunately for me, one of our assistant managers had decided to work the midnight shift and witnessed Tony's negligence. The assistant manager was livid: he fired Tony on the spot. As it turned out, I had missed an opportunity to enforce my values.

That incident taught me that you can't depend on someone else to be around when an unethical situation arises. Knowing what is right is fine, but that knowledge alone is ethics without power.

By not reporting Tony's theft, I was guilty of passive ethics. My ethical thoughts had no impact whatsoever. Only active ethics can alter a situation—as evidenced by the assistant manager who fired Tony.

A dynamic code of ethics may, in the short term, be unpopular and unprofitable. Taking action to right wrongs makes some people uncomfortable. In the long run, however, it increases the bottom line, strengthens the corporate culture, and propagates the values that keep our society safe, stable, and democratic.

9

Open the Kimono!
The Ten Commandments of
Crisis Communication

Open the kimono means "lay yourself bare." Let everyone see your cards—and let them know how you intend to play the game. As far as I'm concerned, there is no better way to describe this productive style of communication. Such an approach is essential in times of crisis.

Eighteen months into my tenure at Southwest, the International Association of Machinists (IAM) union threatened to strike. The union demanded a compensation package comparable to the one that had recently been negotiated at Continental. Such a package may have been appropriate elsewhere, but it simply did not make sense for Southwest.

Our management team made several offers, all of which were turned down flatly by union leadership. Less than ten days before the strike was to commence, I decided to open the kimono. I let every Southwest employee know exactly where both the union and the airline stood on the issues. I also expressed my personal feelings as CEO.

I drafted a three-page letter to IAM union members and a second letter to all Southwest employees and their families. Both letters went directly to people's homes.

The first letter, sent to union members, detailed the negotia-

159

tions between Southwest and the union leadership. In simple terms, it outlined the future of the airline and IAM employees should union leadership continue what I considered to be its stonewalling tactics. The second letter explained to all employees the consequences of Southwest's and IAM's not coming to an agreement. I included a copy of the letter to IAM members with the letter that was sent to all Southwest employees. What follows are highlights of the first letter and the complete text of the second:

TO: SOUTHWEST MECHANICS, CLEANERS, STOCK CLERKS, AND THEIR FAMILIES

Oftentimes, communications get twisted, sometimes by mistake and sometimes intentionally. I felt an obligation, at this time, to be certain that you folks had all the facts so that you can make an intelligent decision—assuming that your union gives you another opportunity to vote before it is too late.

We have been trying to reach an agreement since July. Our initial offer would have cost the Company $1.1 million, over the three-year period, in additional compensation and benefits to you. Your leadership flatly turned it down, pointing only to the Continental Airlines' contract—whose cost was an additional $2.1 million over three years—saying it was that or nothing. We continued to talk and, just before Thanksgiving, the Company again made an offer which would have cost $1.3 million in additional compensation and benefits. You voted that one down 78 to 1. At that point, mediation and negotiation ceased and the thirty-day countdown began.

Fortunately, many of you who helped start and build this Company do not want to strike. Several mechanics with calm, cool heads visited Mr. Vidal and me recently and told us what was important to you. I, in turn, explained to them the Company's philosophy and what we could do. They told us it was extremely important that the mechanics receive a certain minimum base pay during the first year of the contract. They said if the Company could do that, less could be accepted in other areas, such as cost-of-living allowances and health and retirement benefits.

Part of this discussion focused on the Company's ability and need to contract out our fueling operation at Love Field. We have an opportunity to activate the underground hydrant system, which must be operated by Allied. By doing this, the mechanics would be able to devote all their time to maintenance and push-back activities, and we would be able to eliminate the constant problem with the fuel trucks in that operation. We also agreed not to furlough any mechanics because of this change. The Company followed through and presented the proposal when we met last week with your committee.

Not only did your leadership flatly turn this offer down on the spot, they also backed off discussions on no additional cost-of-living allowances and the right to contract fueling. From my perspective, these negotiations have been a one-way street for six months.

Should there be a strike, the Company plans to continue to operate—assuming that enough employees cross the picket line. Those nonstriking employees will all be offered jobs at their normal pay when they show up for work.

Should not enough employees cross picket lines, we will have to shut the Airline down entirely. How long can we afford to be on strike? We can sustain a very long strike if we have to. However, it will mean putting nearly all 1,600 employees on the street without pay. It may also mean not accepting new airplanes and possibly selling existing airplanes. It will mean that when the strike is finally consummated, we will need fewer employees to run the Airline. So you should not expect to be called back to work immediately, if and when a settlement is reached.

No employee at Southwest is paid on a parity with a Braniff or an American—large airlines that have been in business for nearly fifty years. If Southwest were to take on the cost structure of an American and if we were to lose our productivity, we would then have to raise our fares to the same level as American. At that point, many passengers would no longer fly. Instead, they would go back to the automobile or stay home.

All of our routes are short-haul. We do not have a Dallas-to-London or a Dallas-to-Honolulu to subsidize our short-haul routes. Therefore, we would lose our niche in the market and very probably go out of business.

Some of you may be saying, "This is an exaggeration. He is trying to scare us." I can tell you, my friends, after twenty-four years in the airline industry, that it has happened to carriers and it could happen again. The profits at Southwest are not a secret or mystery. They are used for stockholder dividends, for purchasing new aircraft and facilities, and for profit sharing for all of us. At 12:01 A.M. Sunday, January 13, 1980, you have a legal right to strike under the Railway Labor Act. At that time, we will have used up all the mediation and countdown period available to us. The Company plans to honor that strike date.

What does that mean? It means that you will not be allowed on Company property from then until a settlement is reached, however many weeks or months that may take. It also means that you will go off the payroll in every respect.

At that moment, all of your benefits will cease. You will not be eligible for any passes or reduced rates on Southwest or any other carrier. All of your life, accident, and health insurance—plus maternity and dental benefits for yourself and your family—will cease. Since you won't be drawing a salary, you will also not be adding to or participating in profit sharing during the strike. The Company does *not* want a strike, but your union leadership and your employee committee have left us with no choice.

I hope that you have enough pride in your Company and enough respect for your fellow employees, your families, and our customers to seriously consider any action you may take before actually taking it. You should also remember that the executives of the IAM union will continue to receive their salaries while you are out on the street. Be certain in your deliberations that your union leadership truly has your interests—and those of the Company—in mind.

So that your fellow employees may also be informed and have an opportunity to judge both positions, I am sending a copy of this letter to every Southwest employee.

Sincerely,

Howard D. Putnam

TO: SOUTHWEST EMPLOYEES AND FAMILIES

The attached letter has been sent today to all mechanics, cleaners, and stock clerks at their homes. I wanted to share it with all of you also. If we have to shut down the airline at 12:01 A.M. Sunday, January 13, nearly all employees will go off the payroll within forty-eight to seventy-two hours. With no revenues coming in, we cannot sustain our present costs.

We have a plan to fly at least twelve planes, all 737s. All employees except IAM mechanics, stock clerks, and cleaners will report for their normal shifts after the strike begins and will be paid for work performed. If we are operating, you will be guaranteed your normal salary for the next sixty days. What happens after that will depend on our loads and the success of our reduced staff of management and maintenance people. We believe we can do it. I certainly hope so, because I'd hate to see 1,495 of you suffer for weeks and months should the IAM group strike us.

Once we go beyond the sixty-day period, if it becomes necessary and we are still operating, we will endeavor to arrange shorter work weeks, fewer trips flown, or even reduced wages in order to keep all of you on the payroll.

All the officers appreciate your loyalty and understanding during this difficult period for the Company.

Thank you.

Sincerely,

Howard D. Putnam

The IAM was furious that I sent a letter directly to the homes of our employees. I reminded them that these individuals worked for us—not the union. As it turned out, 99 percent of the non-striking employees crossed the picket lines.

For the first two days of the strike we reduced our schedule of flights by 50 percent. Slowly we increased the schedule until employees unaccustomed to certain responsibilities were more comfortable with them. From the initial reduction in service at the onset of the strike, Southwest grew stronger—not weaker.

By the sixth day, the striking employees were anxious to return to work. They accepted our prestrike offer, and we welcomed them back. To celebrate, Southwest threw a huge party at our maintenance base in Dallas.

Approximately one year later, the maintenance employees voted the IAM out as their elected representatives and joined another union.

I feel that our response to this strike, as expressed in these two letters, embodies ten key precepts of good communication. In times of crisis, these guiding principles become imperatives.

The Ten Commandments of Corporate Communication

1. Stay visible.
2. Create an appropriate context.
3. Always be open and honest.
4. Say it simply.
5. Be timely.
6. Act decisively—and with a sense of immediacy.
7. Inform and educate.
8. Be constant.
9. Be receptive and responsive.
10. Speak with one voice.

These principles worked when I managed relatively small crises at Southwest and survived large crises at Braniff. Their value for you is equally great, regardless of whether your company is facing a critical situation at the present time. In fact, by using these canons of communication, you will be creating an effective shield against impending crises.

STAY VISIBLE

Communication during crisis begins with visibility—both in your style of leadership and in the way announcements are made. Announcements and communications that are posted on a dark wall in a forgotten corridor or tucked away in a rarely accessed electronic file will be weak and ineffective. Communication during crisis needs to be bold.

You will note that, rather than posting the above letters on a bulletin board in a common area, I sent them directly to the homes of all Southwest employees. This was not an isolated action but one that expressed my larger commitment to visible management in both good and bad times.

Each day at Southwest, members of the senior management team talked with and listened to employees. Sometimes these were casual encounters—in the hall, in the employee lounge, after hours, or on the way home. On other occasions, these interactions were formal—an appointment, a meeting, a business dinner. Because of this extensive contact with our employees, we often nipped potential problems in the bud.

Visible management and visible communication are essential ingredients of a management style that is participatory and interactive. This kind of approach gives employees a sense of involvement in determining their destinies within the company. When all employees share this feeling, they see their own fate as being wrapped up with that of the company. This perception translates into a more highly motivated and productive workforce.

We kept management accessible. Any employee was welcome. Almost every day, there were three or four employees who, after business hours were over, stopped by to make a suggestion, offer an observation—or just visit. At times, this open-door policy may cause unnecessary interruptions, a little confusion, or a small delay in accomplishing a task. In the long run, however, visible communication in the form of face-to-face interactions between members of a company is beneficial and empowering—to the parties involved and to the company as a whole.

When a leader shrouds himself behind a desk or office walls, when he sends weak and detached messages of leadership, when he uses a spokesperson to talk with constituents instead of facing them himself—these are signs of what can only be described as a closed and cowering management style. In times of crisis, reticence and detachment are unproductive at best. Such situations cry out for visible leaders who are bold and direct.

CREATE AN APPROPRIATE CONTEXT

During a crisis, you must frame your communications within a proper setting. When a situation is critical, emotions run high, attitudes are easily influenced, and opinions are erratic. The opportunity for misinterpretation and misunderstanding is great.

In times of crisis, it is important that you communicate within a framework that surrounds and supports the essential message. The best way to make a difficult statement palatable and understandable is by offering broad-scope and long-term perspectives.

Never convey a message in a void. Barren statistics and figures are often frightening and misleading. Simple statements without appropriate explanation can seem cold and unfeeling. It's important to create a framework that places your words and numbers into a meaningful perspective.

What I said to IAM members, their families, and all Southwest employees could have been expressed more bluntly. I could, for example, have said, "If the IAM union does not capitulate to Southwest's offer, the airline will close down, and we'll all be out on the street." But what purpose would have been served by sending that message?

The intent of the messages in both letters was the same—to jolt the concerned parties into taking a serious look at the situation. If I hadn't created the proper context, however, my intent might have been lost in the emotions of the moment. Without the proper context to guide the trajectory of a message, its impact can be counterproductive. When the proper framework for understanding is lacking, the chances for compatibility between the intent of a message and its impact are slim indeed.

ALWAYS BE OPEN AND HONEST

I have seen many business leaders suppress their thoughts and feelings in the face of crisis. This is a serious mistake. Openness and honesty must begin with the CEO—and include not only the circumstances surrounding the situation but the sentiments as well.

With the two letters to Southwest employees, I laid the facts— and my feelings—on the table. As their leader and a fellow Southwest employee, I expressed where the company stood and where I stood. Later, during Braniff's crisis, I found that openness and honesty helped us reach a faster and more satisfactory resolution.

To deny our emotions is to operate from a position of weakness. Very few things are more powerful than a full disclosure of all factors—particularly those surrounding a crisis.

Effort expended to support untruths or to repress feelings is energy that could be channeled toward resolving a situation. A leader who communicates facts and feelings openly and honestly creates a far more credible perception than one who holds back facts and suppresses feelings. Feelings should not go unchecked and unrestrained, of course, but more favorable results occur when business leaders recognize and declare their feelings.

In the short term, open and honest communication can be embarrassing, painful, and sometimes even counterproductive. In the long term, however, such obstacles should be viewed as necessary steppingstones in the evolution of change through communication. Old barriers must be broken down before new ground for communication can be built—even if this causes a degree of conflict and discomfort for a time.

In the final analysis, full disclosure almost always proves to be the most beneficial course. As far as I'm concerned, deception, for any reason—whether in business or elsewhere—is an unacceptable breach of integrity.

In Chapter 8, I told the story of the Dallas news reporter who asked whether I could guarantee Braniff would be around the following year. Of course I couldn't offer that kind of assurance— and I said so. Some observers think I should have lied. Others have gone so far as to say that my honesty destroyed the airline.

This became an issue of debate in the newspapers and a case study at the Harvard Business School.

I have no doubt that my forthright answer may have caused some additional turbulence for Braniff, but only temporarily. The bottom line is that the airline flew again—and it flew with dignity. I strongly recommend that you always tell it like it is— particularly during times of crisis.

SAY IT SIMPLY

Marty Leaver, former director of public relations at United, gave me my first solid lesson in communication.

"If you are going to say something to somebody," Marty used to counsel, "know what you are going to say ahead of time, and state it succinctly. Get to the point. If you don't know the answer to a question, say, 'I don't know' and promise to get back to the person who asked it."

Get to the heart of the matter when you are communicating— and get there without jargon, convolutions, euphemisms, legalese, or doublespeak. Also, make sure you keep the saccharin and the static out of all your communications.

As I pointed out in the previous section, it is essential to create the proper context. All messages need a supportive environment—but be certain that the support is not gratuitous or superfluous. Make sure what is said does not get lost in what has been left out.

During a crisis, there is little time for writing or reading complex or highly technical language. Yet many officers, executives, and managers feel that they must express even the simplest message in legal, financial, or other obscure terms. The rationale often forwarded for this cumbersome approach is that these spokespersons want to protect themselves or their companies from lawsuits.

Unfortunately, we live in a litigation-happy society. The fear of legal backlash is reasonable—particularly during times of crisis. Nevertheless, I believe it to be greatly exaggerated.

If your intent is to involve others—to pull people together— your message must be honest, simple, and of value to those it is reaching. You can't expect employees to rally behind a cause, idea, or goal that they do not understand. Nor are they likely to marshal their forces if deception is suspected.

The letters I sent to the IAM members and the other Southwest employees could have been laden with legal rhetoric in an attempt to intimidate. They could have been bloated with puffery in an attempt to impress. They could have been embellished with eloquent sweeteners in an attempt to charm and bamboozle. Instead, we laid out the situation in simple everyday language. Our intended messages came across because language was not used as a barrier to communication—as it so often is.

Critical situations are difficult to manage. What is the point of cluttering and complicating issues with obscure, highfalutin', and ambiguous language? Communication is meant to forward understanding and positive action. Simple messages create clear paths for both.

BE TIMELY

During a crisis, tell people what they need to know—when they need to know it. The letters to Southwest employees were not sent after the fact. The input they offered and the responses they evoked would have made no difference then. Nor were the letters sent during the early stages of negotiation. At that point, they would have had little urgency and even less impact.

I sent the letters at a time when they could create awareness and generate a response that would benefit the entire company—a response that would help bring the situation to a satisfactory conclusion. Although it is important to point out the relevance of a particular situation to each individual and its role in his or her destiny, it is essential to involve all employees—as a collection of individuals—in understanding their investment in its future.

In a climactic period, a well-timed communication creates urgency—and is an effective tool for resolving conflict. When a company is experiencing a healthy growth period, timely dissemination of data, information, and knowledge can help ensure that it will remain productive and profitable. When a company is in a state of turbulence, timely communications can help restore order and prosperity.

In discussing the importance of timing and timeliness, we must consider the immediacy of our highly technological global society. We live in a world where communications are instantaneous. Events of significance are available via electronic media within minutes—sometimes within seconds—of their occurrence.

A chemical leak in Bhopal, a nuclear explosion in Chernobyl, an oil spill in Alaska—all become known to the local, national, and global public within an astoundingly short time frame.

Nowadays, such information can spread around the world before it reaches the people in the concerned entity—whether a corporation, a community, or a nation. The media, as watchdog and harbinger, have instant access to hundreds of millions of people around the world. This capability adds turbulence to an already unpredictable environment.

Announcements of tainted products, new products, mergers, acquisitions, and corporate improprieties affect the short- and long-term destinies of companies. Leaders must be able to communicate rapidly about all matters that affect the reputation and competitiveness of their companies. Delays create suspicion— and suspicion undermines credibility. In times of crisis, this can be deadly.

ACT DECISIVELY—AND WITH A SENSE OF IMMEDIACY

Critical situations create their own urgency. As a crisis escalates, the amount of urgency that is generated can become too much for some people to manage. Under such circumstances, responses are often misdirected; actions tend to be inappropriate.

The more pressing the crisis, the more important it is to communicate in a way that forwards what needs to be accomplished as rapidly as possible. Always be aware of your intent *before* you communicate. A strong message of intent will go a long way in creating a sense of urgency on the part of the receiver without generating undue fear.

Good communication always has a reason and a purpose: it relays pertinent information or the translation of ideas. It edifies or enlightens—and sometimes it entertains. In a fast-changing world, there is no time for wrapping important information in small talk.

The letters to Southwest employees concerning the pending IAM strike urgently requested them seriously to consider the possible outcome of contemplated actions. Those letters were filled with the kind of intent and urgency that turns communication into positive movement.

INFORM AND EDUCATE

In times of crisis there is often little time for explanations. Unfortunately, this is when the need for accurate information is most vital. In order to endure and overcome crisis, people need new information, new skills, and new paradigms for understanding and action.

Don't clutter communication with unnecessary data—but do focus on information that educates and enlightens. Remember, people need pertinent and applicable data if they are going to make informed decisions and take appropriate steps.

Before I wrote those letters, few IAM members at Southwest knew the details of negotiations between their union leaders and management at the airline. At the same time, few Southwest employees realized that the strike potentially placed at risk all their jobs—and the very future of the airline.

People often have surprisingly little knowledge about the overall condition of the company they work for. To the extent that they are informed, the perceptions of employees—particularly during crises—tend to be at odds with what the media or corporate spokespersons are saying. More often than not, management hasn't taken the time to inform employees about what is going on.

Since a company's employees are generally the people who are most affected by its decisions, I consider it dishonest not to tell them what is taking place—particularly during difficult times. When you keep people in the dark, you make it impossible for them to make decisions that can benefit themselves, their families, and their companies.

BE CONSTANT

Constancy in communication is one foundation for creating a trusting relationship with employees. The trust developed during good times can help buoy relationships during difficult periods—

as long as the flow of information continues to be accurate and reliable. A company's leaders must talk to and interact with employees on a regular basis.

Constancy builds security—which enables people to act decisively and independently. When an individual knows that she will be informed of decisions or policies that affect her well-being, she becomes motivated and empowered to make positive contributions. If, on the other hand, that individual must dedicate time and energy to uncovering all the facts pertaining to the situation at hand, very little can be accomplished.

The letters I sent to IAM members and all Southwest employees were designed to inform them about matters that were highly relevant to their individual and collective futures. In order to make an informed decision, employees needed this information. Had I not written those letters, they probably would have remained unaware of all the pertinent facts, and who knows what would have happened.

On a day-to-day basis, trust grows from simple but regular communication. If your company produces a daily newsline, make sure that it comes out every day—even if it says nothing consequential. If you produce a monthly newsletter for employees, issue it every single month. If you have scheduled regular corporate or regional meetings, make certain that those meetings take place—even if the thrust of your message is that there is nothing substantially new to report.

Constancy creates credibility and stability—as well as a foundation for trust. Trusting relationships can be a great source of strength—but they must be nurtured continually. During good times, there is an opportunity to solidify these relationships through an open and vigorous dialogue. During turbulent times, those same affiliations need to be handled with kid gloves. In either case, there must be a constant flow of communication based on a mutual give and take between a company's leaders and the rest of its workforce.

BE RECEPTIVE AND RESPONSIVE

Listening constitutes half of the communication process—the more important half! The most essential attributes of a good listener are receptivity and responsiveness.

Because listening is an active process, it's important to listen within the context of who is speaking and what is being spoken about. Listen openly and honestly. Try to eliminate personal agendas from your thoughts. Listen simply and plainly. Avoid complicating what is being said with personal definitions and interpretations. Rather than making assumptions, ask questions that will help you learn more.

There are times when it is especially critical to listen—even though other pressing matters may be vying for your attention. On other occasions, if, based on thoughtful listening, you recognize that time is being wasted, don't hesitate to exercise your option to firmly but politely cut short superfluous conversations.

Everyone who speaks to or corresponds with you has a purpose. For various reasons, however, that person may be unable or unwilling to articulate his or her motive. By listening well and asking appropriate questions, you can find out what people have on their minds.

As much as possible, try to listen with an informed and educated ear. If the communicator speaks of a subject that is foreign to you, try to find a common ground based on mutual need. Even if the discussion revolves around an unfamiliar subject, a skilled listener can offer insight that helps the speaker articulate his or her purpose.

Listen constantly: make it a conscious part of your daily agenda. Keep the doors of communication open. If a situation does not warrant a conversation or your personal involvement, say so. But at the same time make it clear that you are always available when needed.

Too often, especially during crisis, leaders forget to listen. The letter I wrote to IAM members showed a willingness on my part to keep the lines of communication open. As an indication that Southwest was receptive to the needs of IAM members, I responded with the best offer the airline could afford. In contrast, the union's response was stonewalling.

When I arrived at Braniff, I sensed a strong and determined spirit among employees, but morale was low. It was clear to me that these folks felt deceived by management and that they believed, with some justification, that they had gotten the short end of the stick.

Braniff employees expressed their dissatisfaction in a variety of ways: some were rude with customers; others pilfered liquor, freight, and the contents of luggage. I believed that most of these employees were basically honest men and women. Nevertheless, they were able to rationalize their behavior as a justifiable response to unfair pay cuts. After all, they reasoned, management was stealing from them. Didn't that justify their trying to get even?

By the end of my second week at Braniff, I realized that something needed to be done—and fast. I called noted industrial psychologist Dr. Don Beck and asked him to take a look at Braniff's employees, its customers, and the image it was presenting. After he had a sense of what our needs were, Don and I would sit down and work out a way to involve the employees—to make them realize that they had a stake in the airline's continued survival.

Don Beck flew the airline regularly for the next five days. In the process, he talked to dozens of employees and customers. His findings confirmed my suspicions. Even though our management team was working fourteen-hour days and seven days a week trying to keep the airline flying, employees felt that we no longer cared. We felt that we had taken steps to communicate with employees all over the world. We had, for example, sent several videotaped messages to all 10,000 employees in North America, South America, and Europe. Apparently this was not enough.

Don suggested that I write a letter to all 10,000 Braniff employees, explaining the situation from a personal point of view. In that letter, I told employees that I left my comfortable position at Southwest because I believed that Braniff was a great airline—one that deserved to fly. The letter made it clear that I was reaching out for help. I tried to create a sense of urgency by explaining that headquarters needed to know, as quickly as possible, what could be done to improve, change, or restructure Braniff.

Before sending off the letter, I asked Don how many responses I might reasonably anticipate. Don said that, based on his experience, we should expect no more than 500 responses from 10,000 contacts. I decided that if we were going to receive only 500 responses, I would add a postscript to the letter. This stated that any and all employees who took the time to write a reply offering constructive suggestions for change would receive a personal, signed reply from me expressing my thoughts about their suggestions. The only stipulation was that they had to sign their name.

Over the next three weeks, 3,000 responses flooded in: 30 percent of the employees took the time to write to me with their thoughts and ideas. In order to fulfill my promise, I started carrying a notepad everywhere I went—in my office, at home, in the car, even in the men's room. It took nearly four months, but I eventually wrote a personal reply to every one of those employees who had written to me.

My sincere two- or three-line replies had more impact than the original letter. Many employees carried these notes with them and enjoyed showing them to family and friends—even customers. It made them feel good to know that, even in a time of crisis, their suggestions were important enough to warrant a personal response from the president of the company.

I believe that my willingness to acknowledge and respect the opinions of my people set a pattern for recovery at Braniff. When the employees realized that the president of the company was interested in what they had to say, they had tangible proof that their leadership cared. This produced a sense of teamwork that soon spread to our customers—and eventually to the general public. It seemed as though everyone wanted to be part of the team that was going to save Braniff.

Eventually the airline did file for bankruptcy. Nevertheless, because management was so receptive and responsive to the needs and wants of all Braniff constituents—employees, lenders, shareholders, and customers—no joint-action lawsuits were filed against the airline. This is remarkable in the face of a $1 billion bankruptcy.

SPEAK WITH ONE VOICE

During a crisis, every constituent group and every individual needs to receive a consistent message from those who speak on behalf of the company.

We've discussed how important constancy in communication is in building credibility. For such continuity to be effective, it must be administered by a management team that speaks with one voice.

Too often, the leaders of companies in crisis do not concur in their understanding and interpretation of key issues. The CEO is interviewed by the media and says one thing. A vice president is interviewed on another occasion and offers a completely different reply to the same question. A few days later, a third executive offers yet another explanation. When too many voices forward divergent viewpoints during crises, the sense of chaos deepens and the situation deteriorates even further.

At both Braniff and Southwest, mine was the voice that addressed key issues—particularly at critical times. To the extent that other senior officers spoke, their thoughts and words were almost always in synch with mine. This consistency did not come about through rehearsal of a party line. It was, rather, the result of a leadership style that encouraged teamwork and an open exchange of ideas.

*   *   *

As you think about these ten commandments of communication, consider what happens when they are ignored or not applied intelligently. When communication fails, the link that connects a company's goals and their implementation quickly deteriorates and can break entirely. Flexibility and adaptability disappear— and there is no vehicle for constructive change. As a result, turbulence turns to chaos—and the wheels that propel a company's forward movement grind to a halt.

How to Make Your Communications a Two-Way Street

One question I am often asked is, "How can I communicate more effectively?"

The anxiety I often sense underlying this question indicates that many people believe that communication is a mysterious process—one that is hard to master. But in fact simplicity is the essence of communication. A willingness to try is half the battle. The other half comes with using the common-sense principles we have been discussing. In order for the process to begin, however, someone has to speak, and someone else must listen.

It's important to remember that communication is not merely a matter of words. Often action (or lack thereof) communicates more than words do. That's why it's essential that all of your messages—both verbal and nonverbal—support each other.

In recent years, for example, Johnson & Johnson's claims of integrity and concern for its customers was supported by the immediate removal of a potentially tainted product from the market. On the other hand, Exxon's claims and actions during the 1989 Alaska oil spill were incongruent. As a result, the public was more impressed by that corporation's lack of positive action than by its noncommittal words.

Bureaucracy grows where communication has died. When communication is not present, simplicity is replaced by redundancy and unnecessary complexity. Communication breakdowns lead to losses in sales, increased customer complaints, employee unrest, shareholder anxiety, and a decrease in the quality of a company's products and services.

Eddie Carlson, who was president of United Airlines during my tenure there, had a wonderful device he used to fight bureaucracy and a lack of communication. He called it NETMA. Through the NETMA any employee could contact the CEO or other senior officers at any time. It sat outside Eddie's office, all day and every day.

Because there were so many layers of management at United, employees believed that they could never get their concerns heard by senior management by going through normal channels. The NETMA circumvented the backlog created by bureaucratic protocol.

Eddie checked the NETMA daily. Not only did this foster direct communication with the CEO from any member of the company, but it prompted all officers to engage more frequently in open, honest, and thorough communication with employees— and with one another. If Eddie discovered something through the NETMA that he should have been made aware of by an officer or other senior executive, the responsible party would receive one of his famous handwritten notes on a three-by-five index card— his Ready Eddie.

To avoid being reprimanded, officers and executives made it a point to check the NETMA more frequently than Eddie did. They had learned that it was in their interest to stay informed—and to keep the head man aware of everything that was taking place in the company.

I guess by now you're wondering just what this NETMA was. Well, it was nothing more than a notebook and pen through which the people at United could communicate with their CEO—and with each other. Incidentally, the letters NETMA stand for Nobody Ever Tells Me Anything!

As I noted earlier, communication problems also arise when people don't listen. This is the flipside of what Eddie Carlson was trying to fight at United.

When I had the opportunity to lead companies, I sometimes encountered executives who accused me of not keeping them informed. To counter these charges, I came up with my own little book-and-pen device, which I called an ITYBYDL. In it, I logged all the critical information I had passed on to officers or executives—as well as the dates and locations of where the interactions took place.

Whenever one of these officers or executives claimed I had not told them an important piece of information, I would first consult my ITYBYDL. If it was not there, I apologized and promptly relayed the information in question. If it was there, I handed them the ITYBYDL. The letters stand for I Told You But You Didn't Listen!

10

To Save or Not to Save: What to Ask before Attempting to Give a Company CPR

People who have been part of a successful organization that goes from year to year without experiencing a major crisis tend to give little thought to what they would do in conditions of adversity. Let's face it: few people like to pay attention to the what-ifs of life. Many of us go for years assuming that we are lucky enough to avert misfortune. Somehow we convince ourselves that automobile accidents, earthquakes, and serious illnesses are tragedies that happen to others—not us.

In the same way, when business is going well, we become so involved in our day-to-day tasks that we often fail to see or believe the warning signs that are in front of our noses. As we function as if all is well, bigger and bigger chinks in the armor begin to develop—and the winds of turbulence seep through. One day we wake up to find that our once solid and reputable organizations are on the brink of disaster.

By the time a company's leaders recognize the crisis in their midst, it is often too late to implement the kind of contingency plans that should have been put into place while the organization was still relatively healthy. Nevertheless, positive steps can be taken to turn a floundering company around—or, at the very least, to minimize the impending damage.

This process begins by asking a series of probing questions—many of which we explore in this chapter. Your honest and thoughtful answers form the basis of a portfolio of facts and feelings that will help you determine whether it is worth investing your time and energy trying to save a company in crisis.

This is precisely the decision Phil Guthrie and I faced when we were asked to leave a healthy and thriving Southwest Airlines in order to face the considerable challenge of trying to save an almost-defunct Braniff.

While at Southwest, I was spectator to Braniff's demise. Through the 1960s and 1970s that airline was flying high. It was innovative and aggressive and had a flair that characterized the state of Texas and many of the companies within its borders. In fact, Braniff was almost as much a symbol of Texas as the Dallas Cowboys football franchise.

Braniff boasted a fifty-year record of growth and prosperity. The airline, started as a small carrier in Oklahoma by brothers Tom and Paul Braniff, had been the first to bring the SST (the Concorde) to Texas. Braniff was a company with flair—with flight uniforms created by the fashion designer Halston and aircraft embellished with a multicolor design by the artist Alexander Calder.

Then, in 1978, the airline industry was deregulated, and Braniff took on a hawkish expansion plan. Under then-CEO Harding Lawrence, Braniff opened service to sixteen new destinations in one day. While others expanded cautiously, Braniff went crazy, planting its flagpole in as many cities as possible, including Birmingham, Sacramento, Tampa, Salt Lake City, Phoenix, and Ontario.

The airline ordered over $400 million of new aircraft in less than a year. Banks and insurance companies were lining up to lend it whatever capital it needed. Everyone applauded Braniff's boldness—its employees, the cities of Dallas and Fort Worth, and the entire state of Texas.

Braniff's style of doing business was typically Texan. It was big-buck, cowboy macho. While the company was busy pulling out all the stops, nobody paused to consider that this approach might backfire. Harding Lawrence told me that Braniff had predicated its expansion on the government's quick reregulation of the industry. The man was risking Braniff's future on his gut feeling that consumers would not stand for the higher prices and disruptions in service a deregulated airline industry would surely produce. By taking on this massive expansion while others were moving conservatively, Braniff would own coveted routes when the government swooped back in and clamped down on pricing.

Unfortunately for Braniff, reregulation never materialized. To make matters worse, interest rates climbed to over 20 percent, and the price of jet fuel skyrocketed. The air-travel market shrank. Suddenly, the future of every Braniff employee was threatened by what was now perceived as the wrongheaded ambitions of a renegade leader who allowed his company to become saddled with far more fat and debt than it was able to carry.

As I've noted in earlier chapters, Braniff possessed corporate amenities like no airline had ever seen: bowling alleys, an olympic-size swimming pool, art collections, golf courses, a 100-room employee hotel, and offices complete with custom furniture. These were Babylonian appointments the airline could scarcely afford even when times were good. Combined with unfettered egoism and ill-conceived routes, these gratuitous perks were Braniff's death knell. It was long past time to start turning things around.

* * *

What follows are the basic questions Phil and I asked before we agreed to accept the challenge at Braniff. In fact, I always consider these factors when I am asked to become involved in a company's turnaround. Because every company has to deal with variables that are specific to its particular set of circumstances, it is impossible to cover in this book all the questions one needs to ask. But those outlined below are the ones I consider to be most important.

I must caution that yes answers to these questions do not ensure a successful turnaround. They can provide, however, a sense of a company's potential for continued survival. I have organized the questions in a systematic manner, which I hope will be helpful. The success a company has in synthesizing this information will depend greatly on the intuition and skill of its leaders.

General Considerations

1. Will the board of directors and investors be supportive?
2. Do the lenders and creditors have a better opportunity for recouping their investments through restructuring than through liquidation?
3. To the extent that government agencies and elected officials are involved, will they support a turnaround?
4. Is there local community involvement and support?
5. Is there customer support?
6. Do employee morale and employee value systems contribute to the company's continued existence?
7. Are the economies that support the entity healthy?
8. Is the industry healthy?
9. Is the competition weak?
10. Does the company have a strong reputation and image in the marketplace?

Specific Considerations

1. Do you have a reasonable amount of time in which to save the company?
2. Is the information on which to base a turnaround thorough and accurate?
3. Does the company currently fill a viable niche? If not, can a new one be found or created?
4. Is the financial condition of the company suitable for restructuring?

5. Are current products and services of high quality?
6. Can you quickly and confidently form a strong senior management team?
7. Are trade suppliers willing to help?

Personal Considerations

1. Do you have a vision for the company?
2. Are you willing to assume the responsibility and take the consequences of either a successful or a failed quest?
3. Are you more interested in *proving* you can turn a crisis around than in actually turning it around?
4. Is your family willing and able to share in the challenge?
5. Are you alone?
6. Are you in good physical and emotional health?

General Considerations

WILL THE BOARD OF DIRECTORS AND INVESTORS BE SUPPORTIVE?

When I met with Braniff's board of directors, I made it clear that I was not interested in priming the airline for a government bailout. If the board was looking for federal charity, they had the wrong candidate for solicitor. In my view, Braniff would either have to emerge as a survivor on its own or meet an unfortunate but deserved end.

Our system of free enterprise is complicated with restrictions. Free trade is a misnomer: trade of any kind is managed in one way or another. Nevertheless, I feel that our economic system offers the finest mechanism in the world for productivity, growth, and creativity. In the United States we have opportunities to succeed as well as opportunities to fail. Both must be respected.

The same system that was threatening to ground Braniff would have to be the one by which it would fly again. Essentially, this is what I told Braniff's board, which agreed that a bailout would not be considered. This decision was also backed by the company's largest creditors.

To further test the support of the existing board, I requested that new members be added—a move the directors had already been considering. It was my feeling that fresh ideas and a new direction were needed at this level. Not wanting to alienate any of the existing members, I explained that bringing in new blood would send a clear signal to both creditors and the general public that Braniff was serious about changing its ways and restructuring its operations.

The board added Walter Mischer, Sr., a talented banker from Houston; Robert Rogers, CEO of a large cement company in Dallas; Robert Folsom, a successful real estate developer and former Dallas mayor; and Paul Gaddis, dean of a local university's business school. Without a board committed to a newly structured and directed entity, there is little hope for its survival, and these four new members greatly enhanced Braniff's prospects.

These reputable men came on with the understanding that they would receive no fees or stipends for their efforts. They wanted to see a great corporation saved for many reasons: the 10,000 employees and jobs across the United States, South America, and Europe; the positive impact Braniff had on the regional economy; and the proud history of the organization. It gave us great confidence and peace of mind to know that prominent and successful men like these cared enough to put their necks on the line with ours.

DO THE LENDERS AND CREDITORS HAVE A BETTER OPPORTUNITY TO RECOUP THEIR INVESTMENTS THROUGH RESTRUCTURING THAN THROUGH LIQUIDATION?

Phil and I were certain that Braniff's present investors had a better chance of recouping their investment through reorganization outside of the courtroom than through bankruptcy or liquidation. We presented our case to the secured lenders who had the largest stake in the company, and they agreed.

The economy was soft at the time. There was no market for used aircraft. If we shut down and put Braniff's ninety jets on the market at the same time, it would greatly depress their value.

We recommended that the best approach would be to quickly

scale down the size of Braniff and its operating costs. One effective approach to solving the complex problems of a floundering company is to think of it as an onion with many layers of skin to be peeled off. Seldom can a company be saved in one sweeping action. Invariably, there are many problematic layers in dealing with issues such as financing, product lines, plants, and people. All of these issues must be approached rapidly but on a step-by-step basis.

In the process of trying to save a company, you can resolve situations one at a time and try to take some of the complexity out of the structure by peeling off some of the layers. If you can do this successfully, you can put an entity in shape for alternatives that are more attractive than liquidation. Then you can turn your attention to finding a new niche.

In Braniff's case, a shutdown and liquidation would have yielded the secured lenders fifty cents on the dollar and the unsecured creditors less than ten cents on the dollar. A long-term workout (and, as a last resort, a formal Chapter 11 reorganization) made the most sense because that option gave lenders and creditors the best chance to recoup their full investments.

TO THE EXTENT THAT GOVERNMENT AGENCIES AND ELECTED OFFICIALS ARE INVOLVED, WILL THEY SUPPORT A TURNAROUND?

During the Braniff crisis we were fortunate enough to have Drew Lewis as U.S. Secretary of Transportation, Lynn Helms as head of the Federal Aviation Administration (FAA), and Dan McKinnon as chair of the Civil Aeronautics Board (CAB). These leaders and their agencies were cooperative and supportive. We also received assistance from the two U.S. senators from Texas, Lloyd Bentsen and the late John Tower. Each individual lived up to his responsibility to serve the public's best interest without a bailout.

My experience has been that public officials and agencies are willing to help entities that are willing to help themselves. Braniff did not run to the government for new laws or a bailout. On occasion we met with agency officials to discuss different issues regarding restructuring—hopefully, without having to draw on taxpayer dollars.

For example, we came up with a creative way to lease our South

American routes to another carrier. With this arrangement, Braniff earned $30 million over a six-year period. Customers received continuity of service from Eastern Airlines, and no tax dollars were used.

Nothing like this had ever been done before. We were exploring new ground in regard to aviation laws and regulations. With the help of several members of Congress and the leadership of CAB chair, Dan McKinnon, we cleared all legal hurdles within four weeks. That's an astonishing pace for government agencies, which are typically bogged down in an administrative swamp. But it can happen when the right agencies and officials are willing to stand behind you.

IS THERE LOCAL COMMUNITY INVOLVEMENT AND SUPPORT?

Texas is known for its spirit. When the Braniff team was down for the count, that spirit was able to uplift the soul of the airline by generously providing encouragement and support. Employees, customers, corporate neighbors, the community, and even the Dallas Cowboys pitched in to save Braniff.

For over twenty years, the Cowboys had been chartering Braniff aircraft to transport the team to their out-of-town games. Shortly after Phil and I arrived at Braniff, an employee proposed that we name an airplane after the Dallas Cowboys. Everyone thought this was an excellent idea, so we created a proposal and presented it to Tex Schramm, president and general manager of the Cowboys organization, and Tom Landry, the team's head coach.

Our idea was to use a 727. We would paint the tail dark blue with a silver helmet and blue star. The windows under the cockpit would be lettered with the Dallas Cowboys's logo. Inside the plane, we would place name tags of the players over the seats, as well as a dedication plaque on the forward bulkhead. Tex, Tom, and the team members delighted in the idea of a Cowboys plane. However, I envisioned a potential downside.

Because Braniff was in such serious financial trouble, I felt obliged to fully apprise Tex and Coach Landry about the possibility of negative publicity should the airline go bankrupt. Tex never even flinched. He said that the Cowboys and Braniff had been partners for twenty-two years. If the Cowboys' logo on the side of an airplane could lend credibility to Braniff and help it through a difficult time, the entire organization was ready to throw its full support behind the idea.

We also used the plane for regularly scheduled flights when the Cowboys were not using it. This turned out to be an effective marketing tool with our customers.

Later that year, Coach Landry asked if there was anything else he could do to help. We suggested that he appear in one of our commercials, and he immediately agreed. The theme of the ad was "The Cowboys and I fly Braniff. Would you join us?" Danny White, a prominent member of the Cowboys, also made free commercials—as did country-and-western singer, Mickey Gilley. The positive effect of all this on Braniff's credibility was immeasurable.

When a company is exhausted and bleeding, odds are it will sink if it is forced to tread water alone. Support from the entire community is essential to revive a floundering corporate resident. But community response like Braniff received is possible only if the company has been a long-standing contributor to the community and a give-give relationship has been established long before a crisis situation occurs.

IS THERE CUSTOMER SUPPORT?

If the spirit of the community is behind an entity, it is almost certain that there will be a customer base to support its renewal.

Braniff had customers who were loyal and enthusiastic about the airline. When a company treats its customers right, those customers will be there to help in turbulent times. When it came to developing a loyal customer base, Braniff was as good as any company I've ever seen.

As a demonstration of their support, several of Braniff's major customers hosted breakfast or lunch meetings at their offices. They invited senior officers, including myself, Phil Guthrie, and Sam Coates, our senior vice president of governmental affairs, to discuss with them the restructuring of Braniff. They made it clear to us that they wanted to help in any way they could.

Charles Terrell, a prominent local civic and business leader, went so far as to purchase $10,000 worth of tickets in advance— to bolster Braniff's cash flow during this difficult time. Charles also used his extensive media contacts to encourage support for Braniff. As a result of his efforts, a wealthy businessman from San Francisco sent Braniff a personal check for $10,000. None of us even knew who this man was. In the brief note sent with the check, he described himself as a concerned citizen who just wanted to help.

Zig Ziglar, the noted speaker and author of books on motivation and leadership, was another loyal Braniff customer. One day, he called and asked if I would like to be introduced to an assembly of 10,000 people attending a one-day motivational seminar in Dallas. This event featured Zig and the nationally syndicated radio commentator, Paul Harvey. Unfortunately, I had a commitment in another city and could not attend. I asked Zig if, instead, he could give several Braniff employees tickets to the seminar.

Zig provided 300 complimentary tickets to Braniff employees and their families. In the course of the seminar, the plight of the airline was mentioned to the Reunion Arena audience. Zig introduced the group of Braniff employees to the audience, who greeted them with a standing ovation for their efforts at trying to save their company.

Paul Harvey was so moved by the experience that, when he returned to Chicago, he delivered a commentary on Braniff's plight. On his syndicated show, "Across America," Paul spoke about the beauty of the human spirit and its ability to endure and conquer hardship.

Customer enthusiasm and involvement resulted in positive publicity that furthered the cause of saving Braniff—at least from the point of view of morale. Public support gave each of us at the airline the personal courage to continue striving for Braniff's rebirth.

During the Braniff crisis I was interviewed on many occasions by the print and electronic media. Several TV shows invited me to participate in panel discussions that focused on Braniff's importance to the economy. David Hartman, then host of "Good

Morning America," interviewed me live on several occasions. This media exposure was an opportunity to speak directly to Braniff's customers and to the general public.

I always was honest with the media. This visibility gave me an opportunity to let people know where we stood—and how much we counted on their help. I believe the candid communication between Braniff and the public helped the airline through its most trying period.

DO EMPLOYEE MORALE AND EMPLOYEE VALUE SYSTEMS CONTRIBUTE TO THE COMPANY'S CONTINUED EXISTENCE?

If you're coming to a crisis situation from the outside—even if it's just from another division of the same company—try to get a gut feeling for what is in the air. Walk through the halls, talk to the secretaries, observe the people on the front line. What kind of energy do you sense? Is it positive, negative, renewable?

I was always proud of the spirit of the employees at Southwest during my tenure there. When I came to Braniff, I was filled with a new pride. It is easy to have great spirit during good times. The true test comes during a crisis. To this day, I have never seen such loyalty and enthusiasm from a company's employees during troubled times.

Many of the employees who greeted me on the day I arrived at Braniff had recently been furloughed. Although they had no jobs, these dedicated men and women were there to volunteer their time and effort—for free. They wanted to see their company get well again. I was moved to see that they still thought of Braniff as *their* company, even though they weren't working at the time. The momentum of the people at Braniff was so positive and powerful that our ability to overcome adversity transcended any rational analysis of the situation.

I believe that when a crisis is approached on a strictly factual basis, without consideration for feelings, positive solutions are going to be much harder to find. Human beings tend to be motivated at least as much by feelings as by cold facts. If the people around you are willing to invest themselves in extraordinary ways, don't reciprocate with only your experience and your time. Invest your whole self.

Even if employees seem to be lackadaisical, I believe that you greatly increase your company's chances of survival and renewal by fully committing yourself—head and heart—to the process. By asserting a positive example, you can alter the feelings and actions of everyone who can participate in catapulting your company over the top.

ARE THE ECONOMIES THAT SUPPORT THE ENTITY HEALTHY?

When a company is in trouble, you can generally point to an accompanying weakness in at least one of the economies on which it relies—whether local, regional, national, international, or global. Braniff was hit not only by increased oil prices, climbing interest rates during expansion, and the firing of all air traffic controllers—but also by a regionally and nationally recessed economy.

Before you can start reviving a company, you must evaluate your short- and long-term financial prospects realistically. It is important to determine what the economic environment will be like when and whether the entity can emerge renewed and ready to pursue business vigorously. Will the reframed entity do business in the same kind of economy that contributed to its troubles? Should the entity change the primary arena in which it does business from local to regional, national to international? Would the entity be healthiest as a global player, or does its real strength rest in the most local of niches? In order to address these questions, a leader must find the balance between where a company best fits and the health of the markets within which the company will do most of its business.

During Braniff's time of trouble, interest rates were at 20 percent. If Braniff had not already exhausted every avenue for capital during expansion, we may have been able to consider borrowing. However, even if capital had been available, the interest payments would have added yet another burden. General stock trading was healthy, but Braniff's stock had dropped from a high of $40 to $3.25 per share. Therefore, an equity offering was impossible. Braniff did not have many economic factors on its side.

IS THE INDUSTRY HEALTHY?

Take a look at your industry. Is it young and vibrant, mature and stable, old and shrinking? Is it cyclical? Where does your company fit into the overall scheme? Was it an old company that evolved as a competitor in a new industry? Does it lack the youthful, innovative spirit it needed to succeed? Or is it a new company unable to develop a foothold in an established industry?

Historically, the airline business is cyclical. It goes through price-sensitive periods characterized by oversupply and weak travel. Then it goes through periods when demand is high and people are willing to pay a premium for a quality flying experience. During its crisis, Braniff was mired in a price-sensitive cycle of the airline industry.

The health of the industry plays a big part in an entity's ability to survive a crisis. Expect the momentum of a young and vibrant industry to buoy your renewal; expect the lethargy of an old and shrinking industry to make your renewal that much slower.

Braniff, even in a down economy and a down industry, was able to raise its passenger load to the highest in the business for a brief period of time. The real challenge was in trying to sustain the company against the turbulence of an adverse economic environment.

IS THE COMPETITION WEAK?

A certain amount of turbulence is going to come from the competition. If your competition is weak, you have a much better chance of regaining a foothold after reorganizing. If your competition is strong, as it was during Braniff's crisis, turnaround will be difficult.

The activities of Braniff's major competitors, particularly

American, had a serious impact on the airline—especially in the final months. American blanketed every one of Braniff's routes. It covered us with competition and cash we could not begin to match. Considerable publicity was also given to alleged illegal competitive practices by American. But that is another story for another time.

When a company first reenters the market—even with new vision and new courage—it is vulnerable. An organization's rebirth is more fragile than its birth, particularly in the face of strong competition.

If the entity is very weak and the competition very strong, the entity might actually be better off in the hands of the competitor. Under such circumstances, you may want to consider reorganization that moves toward sale. Don't waste all your energy waging war on the competition. Fight for your customers, your employees, your lenders, and creditors. If sale or merger with the competition best serves the constituents—consider it seriously.

DOES THE COMPANY HAVE A STRONG REPUTATION AND IMAGE IN THE MARKETPLACE?

A company with a strong image before its crisis has a much better chance of surviving the inevitable trials and tribulations. A strong image and reputation can buoy a company through many of the rough waves. It can generate support from all constituents—as well as from the public and the media.

If a company's reputation is marginal or poor, it will earn little sympathy and support from those who might be able to lend a hand. It may sound cold to say, but companies like these are often better off buried and remembered for their better days.

Braniff had an outstanding reputation. It was known for being ambitious, flamboyant, independent, and successful. Perks included designer uniforms, palatial headquarters, and planes decorated by Alexander Calder. All the above typified the kind of excessiveness that contributed to the company's financial problems. When times were at their toughest, however, this image with customers, employees, and the general public proved to be Braniff's ace in the hole.

Specific Considerations

DO YOU HAVE A REASONABLE AMOUNT OF TIME IN WHICH TO SAVE THE COMPANY?

What kind of time frame are you facing? Do you have ten months of cash on hand or ten days of cash, as we did at Braniff? Does the company have any free assets? Does it own anything that is not pledged to a bank, insurance company, or other creditors? Can it take that asset to the bank and borrow cash against it in order to operate? This capability adds to a company's flexibility and gives it a greater opportunity to restructure or reorganize.

Braniff had much less cash than we had been led to believe by senior management and the board of directors. That fostered many other problems—the kind that surface when a company is in crisis and is cash poor.

How much time are the lenders willing to give you? Do they want the company turned around in six months when it will take at least sixteen? What about the government and the courts? Have they set deadlines that must be met to avoid intervention? Do lawsuits that will divert time and energy from saving the entity loom on the horizon? How many concerned parties share in the vision of a new company?

When a company starts to lose ground, concerned parties tend to become impatient. However, several factors contributed to extending Braniff's turnaround time. Because we were perceived as being sincere about helping ourselves, public support for the airline was high. Because the new vision for the company was realistic, lenders and creditors were willing to work with us. This patience and support on the part of our constituents gave us more time to generate creative solutions to difficult problems.

Ling-Temco-Vought (LTV), a Texas-based company, has been in Chapter 11 for four years as of this writing. Slowly but steadily, it has been working through a reorganization. For LTV this seems to be the appropriate procedure. On the other hand, Eastern Airlines took an unusual tack in early 1990. The creditors had management judicially removed and replaced by a trustee. A few months later, the company was liquidated through Chapter 7.

The amount of time it takes to reorganize an entity depends on the number of layers of problems and expenses that need to be peeled away. After you analyze the situation, try to get as much time from lenders and creditors as you possibly can. It is not uncommon to ask for two or three times as much time to reorganize as your analysis indicates you might actually require.

Most important, a company needs enough time to get through the chaos caused by extreme turbulence. Although the goal is always to make this process happen as quickly as possible, the most expedient time frame could wind up being months—or even years.

IS THE INFORMATION ON WHICH TO BASE A TURNAROUND THOROUGH AND ACCURATE?

Braniff's downward spiral was so rapid that Phil and I had little time to scrutinize the information. If we wanted to accept the challenge of trying to save Braniff, we had to make our decision quickly. This meant we weren't able to dig into the information as deeply as we would have liked.

The most dangerous aspect of taking the challenge of a turnaround is to get in there and find out that the information given was bogus. Due diligence takes time—and unfortunately this is the one luxury most failing companies can least afford.

At Braniff, the air traffic controller strike was affecting the airline more than we were led to believe, creating an unexpected cash problem. In part, because of the chaos, the existing Braniff management did not fully realize its own situation; in part, they gilded the lily to attract us.

Phil and I knew that Braniff was seriously ailing when we decided to undertake the challenge, but we didn't know that it required intensive care. The company was on its death bed. Frankly, I don't think we would have gone to Braniff had we known how tenuous the airline's future was at the moment we were getting ready to walk through its doors. But once we made our commitment, we were determined to give it everything we had.

DOES THE COMPANY CURRENTLY FILL A VIABLE NICHE? IF NOT, CAN A NEW ONE BE FOUND OR CREATED?

Before accepting the challenge to turn around a failing company, you must have a feel for the industry. Such insight generally comes from experience. Statistics can reveal previous successes and failures, but there are always exceptions. If your intuition tells you that this business can offer something valuable, the challenge may be worth meeting head on.

One essential question that you must ask is whether the company currently offers a product or service of long-term value and profitability. For example, because airline travel is an established industry, a carrier can offer long-term value to its customers and long-term profitability to its vested constituents—but only if it is run properly.

Unfortunately Braniff could not pass this test and lost its standing within the niche of high-cost, full-service national and international carriers. We needed to find or create a new niche— and a new reason for the company to continue doing business.

Our vision for a new Braniff was as a simplified, low-cost, low-fare regional and transcontinental carrier. After my experience at Southwest, I believed that a trunk carrier like Braniff could achieve the same kind of success—only on a larger scale.

IS THE FINANCIAL CONDITION OF THE COMPANY SUITABLE FOR RESTRUCTURING?

At Braniff, we initially chose restructuring outside of Chapter 11. In retrospect, however, Braniff may have been past the point of no return. For many companies in crisis, restructuring is not the best financial move. Other options include liquidation, new capital infusion, merger, acquisition by a stronger company, partial sale of assets—or some combination of these possibilities.

After you determine how much cash there is on hand, you can then evaluate whether any assets can be sold for cash without adversely affecting the quality of the operation.

Two other relevant questions are whether you have a good

relationship with the current investors and lenders and whether there is a realistic possibility of attracting new investors or lenders.

When looking at the financials of a troubled company, two red flags signal the need to look deeper. If payments to suppliers are over forty-five days in arrears, those creditors may begin to hold back products; this can create serious problems during a restructuring. If receivables are behind by more than thirty to forty-five days, cash flow will be interrupted. What is the volume of receivables? How much operating capital does that equate to? Is it enough?

Check the typical cost indicators for the company. Are they in line with the industry? What is the percentage of revenue that supports wages and salaries, administrative and operating costs? Are there any anomalies? If you are going to turn around a serious financial situation, you need to know how and why things got as bad as they did. If something just doesn't seem right, don't be afraid to look further.

We broke new ground with Braniff. Only a handful of large bankruptcies had occurred in the immediately preceding years, mostly in the steel and railroad industries. In those days, lenders were not as interested in restructuring as they are today. Many preferred to take their collateral and go home. As I've noted before, Braniff was lucky to have the kind of support it had from all constituencies, or the attempted restructuring never could have taken place. In any case, lenders have become much more amenable to restructuring these days—perhaps because so many of them are in trouble too.

ARE CURRENT PRODUCTS AND SERVICES OF HIGH QUALITY?

How good is the product the company offers? How good will it be after the company has been restructured and reframed? Has the company strayed from what it does best?

Quality is still a priority, even in a crisis. It makes no sense to take a company back into the business of mediocrity, especially if that's what caused its difficulties in the first place. This time, do it right or don't do it at all!

We determined that our new vision for Braniff would be executed with excellence. The Texas Class service we implemented would be characterized by simplicity, convenience, and value for the dollar. Employees would have fun working for the airline, and passengers would have fun flying it. The new products of the new Braniff would match or surpass the quality of any competing product. I wasn't about to use this second chance to position Braniff as a second-rate competitor.

CAN YOU QUICKLY AND CONFIDENTLY FORM A STRONG SENIOR MANAGEMENT TEAM?

How talented, loyal, and energetic are the existing company's senior members? Are they willing and able to contribute substantially to the company's turnaround? Do you have the option to look outside the company for talent? If so, is anyone readily available? If you are coming in from the outside, can you bring someone valuable with you?

The senior management team plays a critical role in turning around a company. The team needs people with guts, insight, ambition, energy, compassion, and stability. The men and women who can successfully meet the challenge are willing to give up comfortable positions at comfortable companies. They are willing to risk their reputations, their pride, and their egos. The men and women you want around you are those who thrive on responsibility, accountability, and service.

ARE TRADE SUPPLIERS WILLING TO HELP?

Within the first week at Braniff, Phil and I flew to Seattle to meet with Boeing. Their help during this critical time proved to be vital. We had lunch in Boeing's private dining room with T. Wilson, chair, Dick Welch, president of the commercial airplane division, and Hal Haynes, chief financial officer.

The five of us sat at a long table with a white linen tablecloth. On the table there were two tall, slender white candles flickering. I remember thinking that it felt like a last supper.

I told T. and Dick of our turnaround plans. I emphasized how important it would be for Braniff to have their support in terms of furnishing service and parts. The two agreed, and Boeing became a staunch supporter throughout the restructuring.

In soliciting help from your suppliers, evaluate key areas of need and cost. These include rent, supplies, parts, service, maintenance, fuel, and raw materials. Talk candidly to the suppliers of these goods and services. Remind them that your business is their business. If your company stops producing revenue, they will be hurt as well. Make your suppliers understand that it is in their best interest to help. Be honest, candid, and sincere. Keep communications open and outgoing. Don't be afraid to make firm commitments. Do whatever it takes to come to an agreement that is win-win. Such negotiations tend to be delicate. However, if you are steadfast in your resolve and sincere in your intent, a mutually beneficial solution can almost always be reached.

Personal Considerations

DO YOU HAVE A VISION FOR THE COMPANY?

As the new leader, the vision you create for the company must be broader than its new niche. This renewed vision must include a new approach to customers and employees—as well as new commitment to shareholders and the financial community. In addition, the new entity must state its commitment to integrity and communication in creating a new, positive image.

This renewed vision must manifest itself in day-to-day thoughts and actions. It must be vibrant enough to carry you, your senior management team, and the entire company through the chaos of reorganization.

ARE YOU WILLING TO ASSUME THE RESPONSIBILITY AND TAKE THE CONSEQUENCES OF EITHER A SUCCESSFUL OR A FAILED QUEST?

The same qualities you look for in the senior management team must reside within you—the suppleness and resiliency to stand strong and yet adapt to whatever circumstances the challenge may present.

Be prepared to deal with all sorts of tensions and conflicts. You will be called on almost daily to make painful decisions. There may well be lawsuits. Reputations will be made or broken. You may feel pride, confidence, and self-esteem on one day, but on the very next day, you may pick up their scattered remnants from your office floor.

When you accept the challenge to turn around a company in crisis, you commit yourself to simultaneously serving and leading all constituents. Not all of us are capable of undertaking such a commitment. I urge you to think hard before making a final decision.

ARE YOU MORE INTERESTED IN *proving* YOU CAN TURN A CRISIS AROUND THAN IN ACTUALLY TURNING IT AROUND?

Proving you can turn a company around is the wrong reason to take on the challenge. In a crisis, more than at any other time, a leader must be dedicated to serving those who rely most on the company's continued viability—its customers, creditors, and shareholders. There will be other times in life for you to prove your mettle. But taking on the challenge of saving a failing company is an inappropriate context for working out personal or professional insecurities.

IS YOUR FAMILY WILLING AND ABLE TO SHARE IN THE CHALLENGE?

Remember: nobody flies solo. When it was time to seriously consider leaving the comforts and success of Southwest for the turmoil of Braniff, the first person I consulted was my wife, Krista. I needed to know whether she was willing to take the risk with me. Before you go a step further, I urge you to consider whether your spouse and the rest of your family are ready to stand with you in taking this considerable gamble.

ARE YOU ALONE?

When my wife agreed to support me in moving to Braniff, I asked Phil Guthrie, my CFO at Southwest, if he would go with me. Years ago, when I moved from United to Southwest, Eddie Carlson—then president of United—gave me a quick, informal lesson in what I think of as CEO 101. The essential message of that lesson was this: never go in to lead a new company alone; take at least one skilled and loyal supporter to stand by your side and work with you in instituting new ideas.

Braniff's problems were many, but its financial situation required an expert. My experience was marketing and general management; Phil was the financial genius. Clearly, he was the person I most needed to come with me.

The Sunday before moving to Braniff, Krista and I asked Phil and his wife over for dinner. I told Phil and Beverly that Krista and I were going to Braniff. We wanted them to join us.

Phil said he had to sleep on it. He said it as a figure of speech, but overnight was all the time I was able to give him. In any case, I felt that an immediate yes or no would be his gut-level answer. I asked Phil to give me his reply by 8:00 A.M. the following day. The next morning he was in my office. He looked at me and said, "Howard, let's do it!"

I would not have moved to Braniff without the support of Krista and Phil. The challenge was great enough as it was. Without their support and presence, it would have been overwhelming.

ARE YOU IN GOOD PHYSICAL AND EMOTIONAL HEALTH?

It is impossible to predict how well a person will hold up in the face of such a formidable challenge. That's why it is important to evaluate your responses to previous situations—particularly those that have generated a good deal of stress. Recognizing and accepting the many different physical, emotional, and spiritual consequences of confronting the adversity you are sure to face in taking on a failing company is a vital exercise. If you conclude that the stress and strain pose a threat to your well-being, seek out other challenges.

* * *

We have been exploring some of the vital questions that need to be addressed before you can begin the process of saving a failing company. In theory, the more of the above questions you are able to answer positively, the more likely you are to overcome the obstacles. The more complete and accurate the knowledge of yourself, the general economic climate, and the company you will be working to turn around, the greater your chances for success.

There are no guarantees, however. That is why I urge you to explore these issues carefully. Look deep and address each question honestly—but try not to take too long. When you are trying to navigate your way out of extreme turbulence, time is the one thing you can't afford to lose.

11

Red Alert:
What to Do When It Hits
the Fan

For years, the airline industry has had emergency procedures in place—both to prevent potential accidents and to minimize the damage of an incident once it occurs. As soon as a flight reports a potential problem, the crew and all units at the destination airport go on ready—or amber—alert. This means that all systems are open and all personnel are standing by to await further word. Everyone has been alerted and is working to diagnose and resolve the problem.

In handling emergencies, airlines operate much like traffic lights—with signals running from green to amber to red. Unfortunately, the amber-alert status does not exist in most companies. When a business is in trouble, it usually goes from green directly to red—thus depriving itself of the opportunity to prepare for emergencies. This is precisely what happened at Braniff.

* * *

Shortly after I arrived in Dallas to take over as CEO of Southwest, the chairperson of a large Dallas bank hosted a reception for several hundred business leaders. Among the prominent members of the local business community who attended was

Harding Lawrence, then CEO of the highly successful Braniff International. Lawrence had led Braniff for over ten years. During that time, it had gone from being a midsize carrier to the sixth largest in the United States.

Texas was in a boom period, and Braniff—the hometown airline—carried a lot of weight both socially and politically. Many of the local entrepreneurs and business leaders identified with Harding Lawrence and linked his success at Braniff with the economic growth of Texas and the entire southwest region.

As the dinner reception neared its end, nearly everyone was gone—except for Harding Lawrence and myself. Apparently, he was waiting around to size up the new kid on the block. He asked a lot of questions about my experiences at United Airlines, and seemed particularly interested in the company's position on airline deregulation.

United had been the only major carrier to endorse deregulation and had led a strong effort to get it approved in Congress. Southwest, as a small intrastate carrier, had also supported deregulation—because without it they were gridlocked in Texas. I remember thinking about how ironic it was that I had gone from an airline that was deregulation's largest supporter to one that was its smallest supporter.

As we finished devouring the remaining shrimp and hors d'oeuvres, Lawrence turned to me and said he was against deregulation. He made it clear, however, that if it occurred, Braniff would expand very rapidly and put their flagpole in as many new cities and countries as possible.

Harding Lawrence felt that the window of expansion opportunities would be short-lived. Furthermore, he did not think the public would benefit from the airline industry's deregulation and that Congress would reinstate regulation in short order. I'll never forget the far-reaching look in his eyes and the determination in his voice as he spoke of his plans.

When I got home that evening, I said to Krista, "If deregulation comes to pass, look out for Braniff." It was obvious that Braniff's CEO had already drafted his flight plan and was ready for a rapid takeoff.

As many of us had anticipated, President Carter soon signed the Airline Deregulation Act. In response, Harding Lawrence

began an expansion plan that would have made Napoleon trem-
ble. As the Civil Aeronautics Board made new routes available,
Braniff filed for permission to service hundreds of new destinations. Within the first thirty days of receiving approval, Braniff
opened service to sixteen new cities; competitors added only one
or two new routes.

Braniff's rapid and short-notice expansion required astronomi-
cal expenditures. Airport leases were negotiated at an accelerated
pace with an exorbitant premium tacked on. Union contracts had
to be amended so that service could be started quickly. This sense
of urgency increased costs while reducing the airline's efficiency.
In addition, many of the new routes had very low traffic volumes.
They were unprofitable from the first day, and their continued
operations had to be justified from headquarters.

To fly the new routes, Braniff had to order new aircraft immediately. Over $400 million was borrowed from thirty-seven
banks and insurance companies to place the necessary orders for
airplanes from Boeing and engines from Pratt & Whitney. As a
result of the expansion, several thousand new employees were
hired to fly the planes, board the passengers, and maintain the
aircraft.

On one level, Braniff was the victim of circumstances. Within
a few short months of its expansion, the economy stumbled, air
travel slackened, jet fuel prices soared, and interest rates bal-
looned to an historic 20 percent. As bad as these setbacks were,
they certainly could have been managed better. Industry analysts
and senior employees cautioned Braniff's leadership that expansion had to be curtailed, but Harding Lawrence did not want to
hear it.

Before long, the effects of turbulence began to manifest themselves. Braniff's once-sizeable profits plummeted into the red.
The chaos of one-man-band, cost-be-damned leadership had
thrown Braniff into a tailspin. Because no mechanism was in
place to signal an amber alert, no preparations had been made to
deal with an impending emergency.

Some saw what was coming. But as so often happens with
autocratic leaders, Harding Lawrence shot the messengers who
tried to warn him that his expansion would backfire. Executives

who did not support his expansion plan were fired or placed in remote areas of the company where their voices could not have an impact. As a result, Braniff went from all-systems-go to red alert with very little time in between.

Is There a Doctor in the House?

Under duress from the Braniff board, Harding Lawrence left the airline. On Lawrence's departure, John Casey, who had been executive vice president of operations, became the airline's new chief executive officer.

Although it is understandable to first look inside a company for new leadership, this is not necessarily a beneficial course of action. John Casey had been with Braniff for thirty years. He was wed to past policies and procedures. Many of the other senior executives were his friends. The decisions he would have to make would be all the more difficult because of his attachments to the past and his long-standing relationships with fellow employees.

John Casey made some tough decisions—but, in retrospect, they were not tough enough. Under his leadership, lenders agreed to a moratorium on interest and principal for several months. Cash flow was increased through several measures, including an across-the-board pay cut of 10 percent. John himself agreed to work without salary for a year. The new CEO also implemented several marketing schemes. Unfortunately, these campaigns lacked continuity and failed to generate any revenue.

Nine months after John Casey took over, little progress had been made—and the bleeding had not been abated. The board and lenders decided that it was time to look outside the company for solutions.

Is There a Telephone in the House?

One day John Casey called and asked me to join him for breakfast. We met at a small restaurant in a Dallas suburb. At first, I thought John wanted to meet to discuss the Boy Scouts of America. The organization is headquartered in the Dallas area, and John was actively involved in its operation. I had hardly finished drinking my orange juice, however, when John unloaded both barrels and asked me to come to Braniff as his chief operating officer. I was stunned.

He was fidgety and full of nervous energy. Clearly, there was more to his request than he was revealing. I later learned that our meeting was prompted by the Braniff board. I was their choice, not John's, to become the airline's COO.

Minutes after returning to my office at Southwest, I received a call from Elvis Mason, then chair and CEO of Interfirst Bank—Braniff's largest lender in Texas. Elvis, an intense and persuasive gentleman, prevailed on me to consider John's offer seriously.

Over the next several days, phone calls and meetings between myself and various members of the Braniff board ensued. The board had been keeping a close eye on Southwest. They liked the simple yet professional management style we had implemented there—a style that produced low costs, high productivity, and an excellent reputation both inside and outside the airline business. Braniff's board members felt that these qualities were essential to a successful turnaround or restructuring.

A few days later, I asked Phil Guthrie to consider coming to Braniff with me. This complicated negotiations for a time, but later the board recognized that Phil's command of finance and our synergistic working relationship were valuable assets.

I soon realized that rather than joining Braniff as COO I should have insisted on coming on board as CEO. The situation at the airline was dire. In order for my presence to have an impact, there would be little time to consult with John on every decision. Moreover, he was often reluctant to support the immediacy and the creativity with which Phil and I were approaching Braniff's problems. I had no choice but to supersede John and talk directly to the board. I explained what needed to be done, and the title of CEO was granted shortly thereafter.

John Casey was deeply hurt by this turn of events. He was displaced to figurehead chair with little influence on the company's day-to-day operation. Several weeks later, he quietly and sadly resigned after a thirty-year career with Braniff. John moved on to work with a former Braniff executive named Eddie Acker, who was at that time CEO of Pan American Airlines.

Taking Control

In a crisis there is one operative philosophy that supersedes all others: take control, and take it fast.

If the board had called me—or any potential new leader—nine months earlier, we would have been in an amber-alert situation, and Braniff probably would not have been forced to file Chapter 11. Procrastination is, by definition, the antithesis of taking control. Nothing is more dangerous in times of crisis. It is far safer to be prematurely preemptive than to fall victim to the typical too-little, too-late actions that are the hallmarks of failing companies.

Flying a company through a storm is accomplished with many of the same things it takes to fly when things are going smoothly: teamwork, simplicity, need fulfillment, ethics, communication, and a sense of urgency. In times of crisis, however, the one essential short-term goal is survival. Without that, nothing else matters.

In certain respects, it is easier to manage in a crisis precisely because the focus is so narrow. The time pressures you are under create their own momentum and urgency, which force you to move fast.

I am often asked what I would do differently if I again faced a situation like the one at Braniff. Basically, I wouldn't change anything in terms of strategy or approach, although I might try to move even faster than I did.

In terms of creating productive objectives in times of crisis, your decisions must reflect a duality of purpose—the mission of survival and the vision of the future. Both need to be forwarded simultaneously. However, the future can only be planned for, not lived in. Survival in the present must occupy every bit of attention and energy an organization can muster.

Phil and I often worked fourteen-hour days and seven-day weeks. This kind of grueling schedule is not uncommon when new leadership is brought in to try to save a failing company.

Although working under such conditions may force you to be decisive at a rate you consider unsafe, there is sometimes no other choice. Looking back, I feel that most of the decisions we made were accurate.

When I became CEO of Braniff, I was free to fully implement a plan for that company's survival. I remember telling Phil that, in a very real sense, we weren't joining Braniff. Instead, we were going to get them to join us. We had been very successful in using the team approach and the other turbulence principles to build Southwest Airlines. It was my intention to use those same precepts and values to meet this new challenge. With the indispensable help of Phil and every Braniff employee, I proceeded to do so. These are the goals we set for ourselves:

- Restructure the company's $600 million debt.
- Find a new niche.
- Reshape the management structure, top down.
- Improve employee productivity.
- Decrease costs.
- Simplify the product for the customer.

Our plan for restructuring Braniff included intense engagement with six specific domains. In describing each of these areas below, I have listed at the beginning of each section some of the specific challenges we faced. Some of these might not directly apply to every business circumstance, but I believe that they are relevant to most crisis situations.

Companies experiencing the chaos of crisis need to focus attention on the issues that follow. At the same time, some energy must be used to nurture the dream for a new entity. A successful quest for survival is almost always driven by the vision of a new and better future that will come to pass after an organization's most pressing needs are addressed.

CAPITAL, FINANCIALS, AND EXPENSES

- Preserve all existing capital, and reduce expense to levels serviceable out of revenues.

- Establish a moratorium on service to interest and principal debt and on debt to trade suppliers. Maintain this state for as long as possible.
- Establish a break-even point based on current revenue and reduced or eliminated expenses.
- Establish rigorous guidelines for accounting, and centralize all authority to spend.

Phil and I understood how important it is to seize control of capital, financial accounting, and all expenses in times of crisis. This was going to be our first step, but when we arrived at Braniff, we received an unexpected jolt. Less than two weeks' worth of operating cash remained. We immediately secured it, and Phil then proceeded to audit all expense categories. Within twenty-four hours, he issued new guidelines as to who could authorize spending. All expense areas were curtailed without delay. Later we froze all budgets, except for payroll.

To strengthen an administrative weakness in accounting, we recruited Steve Turoff, a talented young partner from a Dallas accounting firm, as our controller. We eliminated all discretionary expense areas that did not contribute to the short-term goal of survival, while we nurtured those that affected the company's product and service quality—its lifeblood.

With cash dangerously low, we thought in terms of days, not weeks. Our goal was to push ten days of cash to eleven, then to twelve, then to thirteen. We pushed as far as possible, squeezing receivables to speed up collections, while dragging out payables as long as possible—until suppliers were screaming. At that point, we began dealing with our trade suppliers one at a time. Although we were short of cash, we were long on honesty and sincerity.

The Marriott Corporation was our largest trade creditor. Braniff owed the company $6 million for food and beverage service. As we tightened our belt throughout the organization, Bill Marriott, Jr., the chair of Marriott, called to determine Braniff's status. He wanted his money immediately and was contemplating cutting off service to Braniff.

Half-kiddingly, I told Bill that, with his help, Braniff might set a new trend in the industry—no food service on national flights. He chuckled, but he got my point.

I told Bill that it was not possible for Braniff to catch up on its payments of the $6 million. However, I did promise that the airline could pay as it went for current usage. Bill agreed to the arrangement and wished me luck. Later, Bill Marriott, Jr. was one of the first to endorse my speaking career.

In times of trouble, leaders of companies tend to hide in the bunker and ignore their creditors. I believe such an approach is ill advised. I recommend opening up the kimono. Give your creditors a true and accurate picture of where the company stands. Then request their assistance for the benefit of all. Make them partners in helping you find a workable solution. If you are going to survive a crisis, it is critical that you develop and nurture empowering relationships with all constituents—including suppliers. I have more to say about this later in the chapter.

PUBLIC RELATIONS AND MARKETING

- Establish a crisis-management public-relations plan.
- When the time is right, implement a recovery-and-repositioning marketing campaign.

To manage public relations in times of crisis and to prepare for an eventual recovery campaign, a company's leaders need to have an intimate working relationship with an advertising agency.

The Bloom Agency was Southwest's advertising agency while I was CEO. When I moved to Braniff, the agency wanted to move with me. The risk was high: Braniff had little to spend on advertising; there was no guarantee Braniff would survive to honor any deferred payment; Bloom was almost certain to lose the Southwest account because of a potential conflict of interest.

Tony Wainwright, CEO of the Bloom Agency, and Bob Bloom, the agency's chair, fully understood the risk they were taking, yet they still wanted to help. Before I made the final decision to bring them on board, I set up conditions. Tony, personally, had to be Braniff's account supervisor, and, at least during the most critical periods, he had to spend at least half of his time on our account. To ensure his commitment, we gave him an office at our headquarters and placed him on the Senior Management Committee.

As payment, the Bloom agency would receive a fixed fee instead of a commission. One month we would pay them cash, and on alternate months we would pay in an equivalent amount of free airline tickets. We shook hands and went to work.

In a few days, Tony and his people developed a campaign called, "Braniff Is Going Your Way." It was friendly and powerful, not arrogant and assuming. It set a new tone for Braniff, and the public responded enthusiastically. Informal consumer research revealed that the word on the street was that, although Braniff was under severe financial pressure, the public felt the airline had purpose and hope. The crisis campaign did what it was supposed to—reestablish public confidence in the airline.

As part of our recovery strategy, we dropped first-class service and initiated Texas Class service. This was a single-class, no-frills service designed to give cash flow a much-needed boost. By cutting out such amenities as gourmet meals and replacing them with Texas-style barbeque sandwiches, we reduced prices and increased the number of passengers on our flights. My wife, Krista, came up with the name. When I described the still-unnamed concept to her, she said, "That is truly Texas Class." Everyone at the advertising agency loved the name, so we kept it.

Texas Class service was the right product at the right time partly because it was launched during a period of tremendous statewide esprit de corps. The oil market was booming; real estate and banking were at record highs. Support services and business for these three industries were also remarkably prosperous. All these factors contributed to make Texas Class a hit.

Perception, image, and reputation have an extraordinary influence on the success or failure of any business. In crisis the impact is multiplied one hundredfold—for better or for worse.

SALES AND PRODUCTIVITY

- With break-even established, determine necessary increases in sales and productivity to meet or exceed break-even point.
- Make necessary-increase figures known to every employee.

Increasing sales and productivity may be your most important objectives in trying to survive a crisis. This area is not within direct control of the CEO, so it is often the most difficult to control.

As a rule, a CEO can take direct responsibility for financial matters, public relations, the product line, organizational structure, and constituent relations at the highest directive level. It is difficult, however, to have one-on-one rapport with large numbers of front-line employees—and as I have discussed elsewhere, those folks really make the difference. To some degree, a CEO's influence can be increased by implementing policies and procedures that encourage productivity and performance.

At Braniff we instituted a number of operational changes—including the rescheduling of planes—to reflect our new approach. We also cut the sales force by 50 percent. Such cuts may seem contradictory at a time when a company is attempting to increase productivity. However, reversing the financial fortunes of a floundering company generally means paying full attention to those areas that generate the most revenue and exact maximum productivity from sales personnel. Unfortunately, this often means that some people have to be let go. In order to preserve a sense of harmony among those people who remain on board to implement the new strategy, such cuts must be supported by open and frequent communication between senior management and employees.

During a crisis, the board, the CEO, and the senior management team must be living examples of what is necessary to survive. They must be dedicated, accountable—and, above all, professional. It also is important to always maintain a sense of humor—no matter how bad things get. These are the qualities everyone who works for the company will need to increase productivity to levels that will take the entity from crisis to break-even to growth.

PRODUCTS AND/OR SERVICES

- Establish which products represent the majority of revenue.
- Eliminate all product research and development that is further out than six months.

Depending on the complexity of the business, the 80/20 rule can be a good starting point. Between 10 and 30 percent of the products from multiple-product companies often represent as much as 80 percent of the revenue. Get rid of the 80 percent of the products that represent only 20 percent of the revenue. Then concentrate on upgrading your remaining products to the highest possible quality.

Braniff's product line was out of control. There were 578 fares. One Sunday the senior management team sat down and reorganized the products we offered our customers. In a matter of hours, we reduced the number of fares from 578 fares to just fifteen. We also eliminated first-class service, which cost more to sustain than it earned.

As a result of simplifying our product line, sales increased— while administration, accounting, and customer service became far easier to manage. Because a simpler fare structure was more cost efficient, it ultimately led to lower fares for our customers— much to the chagrin of our competitors. When we eliminated first class, legroom in coach was expanded. This noticeable change in the quality of our product was reflected in sales.

Regardless of the nature of your business, it makes sense to trim and simplify your product or service line, as well as your pricing. Crisis offers a unique opportunity to clean house and fix things that may have contributed to the entity's softness. Here is your chance to discontinue products and services that generate only modest customer interest. There will never be a better time to eliminate those things that are losing money or creating only marginal dollars.

ORGANIZATIONAL STRUCTURE

- Regardless of the size of the organization, start by eliminating no less than 25 percent of senior management. More cuts may be necessary later.
- Establish a commanding senior management team that includes current members of the company mixed with new talent.

- Deconstruct hierarchies of individuals and establish a flattened structure of networked teams.

When I walked through the doors at Braniff there were almost sixty vice presidents. Less than four months later there were just over twenty. At the same time that new talent was being brought in, we reduced total senior management by over 35 percent. Any organization in trouble is too fat—almost by definition. Any organization still ruled by hierarchical forms of leadership is lethargic, antiquated, and incapable of the flexibility it needs to weather the turbulence of a crisis.

On my first day at Braniff, John Casey called a meeting of all officers: it was time for introductions. John stood in front of the group, made a few opening remarks and then introduced me as Howard Swanson—the CFO whom Phil Guthrie had just replaced. There was a dead silence in the audience, as John's embarrassment swelled. He soon realized his mistake and proceeded to correct himself: "Excuse me, ladies and gentlemen, I mean Howard Putnam."

When I stood up I could not resist a chance to inject some humor into the situation. "Thank you, Harding," I said. To many in the room, the reference to Harding Lawrence, Braniff's former CEO, was crystal clear. The entire audience broke into laughter, and a good deal of tension was eased away.

As Alan Stewart, our general counsel, said in private, following the misspoken introductions: "The moment the laughter broke, a new era at Braniff had begun. Everyone recognized that the new team was now in command."

Organizational structures are nothing more than protocols of communication within a group of people. Open the lines of communication, and watch the pyramids crumble. One of a leader's most important jobs in times of crisis is to change the organizational mindset to one that is more empowering. Here are some suggestions for making that happen:

Establish teams linked by a superordinate goal. Operate as a flat structure. Think of the entity as a wheel on its side. The CEO is the hub, and front-line employees are at the rim. Everyone in between are the spokes. This kind of center-out network gives an entity the kind of strength that is missing in top-down hierarchies. Communicate this concept to your people, and set an example in everything you say and do. Remember, perception and behavior determine the kind of structure that characterizes your company.

CONSTITUENT RELATIONS

- Establish an empowering, synergistic relationship based on trust and commitment with all constituents—particularly your employees.
- Open the lines of communication throughout the organization.

Everything in business begins and ends with the employees. Unfortunately, a CEO cannot create rapport with each individual employee, especially in times of crisis. It is possible, however, to speak powerfully through your deeds and gestures.

The Saturday of our first week at Braniff, Phil and I moved into our new offices with the help of our wives, Beverly and Krista. John Casey was there to greet us.

As I have described, the offices were opulent, almost palatial. When John showed us our new offices, they were decorated with Calder paintings, the only art sanctioned by the airline.

When Phil and I entered the office, the first thing we did was to take down the Calders. We felt strongly that it was time to remove the old Buddhas. John was visibly hurt. The symbol of the Calders was as important to him as it had been to Harding Lawrence. John was clearly still part of the old guard, but this was no time for sentimentality. In place of the Calders, Phil and I hung snapshots of our families and photographs of airplanes.

By 9:00 A.M. Monday morning word had spread throughout the Dallas–Fort Worth headquarters that it was now okay to personalize one's workspace. A new friendliness at Braniff was born on that day. The difference could be seen and felt immediately.

Words are important in trying to create rapport with employees, and I certainly did my share of talking. There is no question, however, that what a leader does usually has a far more powerful effect than what he or she says. Action is something that your employees can see and feel.

A company in crisis needs patience, support, and understanding from its constituents. What it must offer in return is honesty and commitment. This kind of give and take underlies a relationship built on trust.

Besides the initial gesture of removing the Calders, I called together the five national unions that represented nearly all Braniff employees. I then proceeded to explain our plan for saving the failing airline.

Some groups were receptive; others were resistant. None was interested in another pay cut, and I did not request one. However, I did request that productivity increase, and I promised that the fat at all levels would be eliminated. This meant 2,000 jobs would be terminated and the employees laid off. I also said the pilot contract, which was due for renewal, would have to be quickly renegotiated to include significant productivity measures.

Finally, I made it clear that if we were going to succeed, all this had to be accomplished in three and a half months. Every person in the room went into shock, but the meeting still wasn't over. I had yet to tell them the conditions under which I came on board to lead their company.

There was no golden parachute in my agreement with the Braniff board. Win, lose, or draw, I gained no more than my salary, the amount of which was public information and commensurate with the responsibilities I had undertaken. If I won, if we turned Braniff into a profitable entity, there would be a cash bonus and stock options. Once the employees realized that my primary goal was to save their airline from folding, not to fill my own pockets while their jobs were on the line, a remarkable energy filled the room. By the time we left that meeting, everybody had committed themselves to a single purpose.

If you are going to survive a crisis, trust must be established quickly between a company's leaders and its most important constituents—employees, unions, customers, lenders, suppliers, shareholders, and the general public. Depending on the current state of relationships, the approach to building this trust must be handled differently with each constituent group. There is, however, one constant that should drive the building of an empowering association with constituents—and that constant is trust.

Get Mad at the Events, Not at the People!

About two weeks after filing for Chapter 11, which was about eight months after we had first stepped foot into Braniff's offices, Phil and I were summoned to New York. The purpose of our trip was to meet with the committee that represented the secured lenders. Together with our attorney, we were driven to an early morning meeting with those lenders at the Union League Club in Manhattan.

Phil and I assumed the meeting was to start the process toward a workable and acceptable plan for reorganization. Breakfast was scheduled for 8:00 A.M., so we arrived at 7:45 A.M. An attendant ushered us into a clubby, high-ceilinged, wood-paneled library.

I sat down, opened my brief case, pulled a memo from inside, and began to read. The attendant, who was still present, walked over and asked me to leave the room:

"In the library," he said curtly, "the only material that is permitted to be read is the material that is already here. This is not a business room—nor is it a meeting room." He then proceeded to escort us to a waiting room. I had never been evicted from a room in which one is permitted to read only specified materials. A premonition of what was yet to come began to press at my gut.

Shortly after 8:00, we were beckoned to the Union League boardroom. It was an immense, lusty statement of wealth, arrogance, and influence. Within its walls were at least forty vice presidents of the major banks and insurance companies that had lent Braniff capital, along with a small army of attorneys and executive assistants.

The group had already finished consuming a full-service breakfast. The smell of fresh coffee and hot Danish pastry still floated in the air. As we eyed the sterling silver utensils and expensive china, the group stood, in unison, to greet us. Their eyes struck us like bullets, and the feeling in the room was one of great intimidation.

Phil and I looked for our seats at the long mahogany table at which the group was seated, but we could not find any empty chairs. Then, at the far end of the room, we spotted a small card table that was at least two inches lower than the imposing conference table from which it was separated. On it there sat three styrofoam cups and several doughnuts on a paper plate. Beside the table were three folding chairs. Obviously, this is where we were to sit.

We quickly sized up the situation and realized this was not a friendly planning session, but a setting for intimidation to let those folk from Texas know who was going to control the reorganization. Our place in the pecking order had been none-too-subtly established.

Phil was muttering some four-letter words through his teeth—none of which sounded like *love*. "Take it easy," I whispered to him. "We've been had, but let's remember to get mad at the events—not the people."

At that point, I began introducing Phil, myself, and our attorney to every single person seated at the table. I shook hands with each vice president, attorney, and executive assistant in the room. By the time I had circumnavigated the table with introductions and finally reached the card table, the man who was chairing the meeting had grown furious.

He was a tall, dignified insurance company executive, and I thought fire was going to come spewing out of his nostrils as he appeared to be losing control. The gentleman proceeded to pound the table with his fists as he launched into a fifteen-minute tirade about the honor of the lenders and the contemptible behavior of Braniff.

"We have loaned Braniff millions and millions of dollars in good faith," he said. "We put our money and our trust in your airline—and this is what it has come to! The only decent thing to do is to give us back all of our airplanes! Without any argument. Thank you."

In all my years in industry I had never heard such childish remarks from a businessperson of this stature. Our attorney gripped my knee for fear I might lose control and jump out of my seat in a defensive rage.

I sat quietly until the speaker finished saying his piece. When he was done, I stood and remarked that I was delighted by the invitation to dine that morning with such a distinguished group. However, I was obliged to inform them that they could not have their airplanes back.

I continued to explain that I was what in legal parlance is known as the debtor in possession. As such, it was my responsibility to treat all creditors and constituencies equally. My job was to do the best I could to reorganize Braniff as soon as possible so that all creditors could benefit. That, I informed my hosts, was precisely what I intended to do.

It took three months to convince the lenders that the new management at Braniff was sincere about treating all concerned parties fairly and justly. Ultimately, we created the trust to proceed, and we began moving rapidly toward reorganization.

Within sixteen months, the $1 billion restructuring was approved by Judge John Flowers in Fort Worth, Texas, and Braniff was ready to fly again under new ownership and a fresh management team. By using the kind of techniques I have described to navigate the winds of turbulence, the red-alert situation at Braniff had been abated—at least for the present.

Index

221

For information on personal speaking appearances, seminars, and consulting, Howard Putnam may be contacted at:

Howard D. Putnam Enterprises
P.O. Box 796336
Dallas, Texas 75379
(214) 985-9827